T0247895

◆ **THE BAD BITCH BUSINESS BIBLE** ◆

THE BAD BITCH BUSINESS BIBLE

LISA CARMEN WANG

10 COMMANDMENTS TO BREAK FREE OF
GOOD GIRL BRAINWASHING AND TAKE CHARGE OF
YOUR BODY, BOUNDARIES, AND BANK ACCOUNT

HARPER
BUSINESS
An Imprint of HarperCollins*Publishers*

THE BAD BITCH BUSINESS BIBLE. Copyright © 2023 by Lisa Carmen Wang. All rights reserved. Printed in the United States of America. No part of this book may be used or reproduced in any manner whatsoever without written permission except in the case of brief quotations embodied in critical articles and reviews. For information, address HarperCollins Publishers, 195 Broadway, New York, NY 10007.

HarperCollins books may be purchased for educational, business, or sales promotional use. For information, please email the Special Markets Department at SPsales@harpercollins.com.

FIRST EDITION

Designed by Bonni Leon-Berman

Library of Congress Cataloging-in-Publication Data has been applied for.

ISBN 978-0-06-320899-5

23 24 25 26 27 LBC 5 4 3 2 1

To my mom, dad, and brother for supporting and loving me from good girl to Bad Bitch and everything in between.

"Who knows what women can be when they are finally free to be themselves."

—*Betty Friedan*, The Feminine Mystique, 1963

CONTENTS

THE TEN BAD BITCH COMMANDMENTS

INTRODUCTION

UNLEASH YOUR INNER BAD BITCH

I spent my entire life feeling like I wasn't enough.

When I got As as a student, I felt like a nerd and hid from the popular kids.

When I won gold as a gymnast, I felt like a target and stayed out of the spotlight.

When I got into Yale, I felt like an imposter and fell silent in class.

When I started working on Wall Street, I felt like a fraud and diminished my value.

When I started fundraising for my startup, I felt like an amateur and settled for less.

Each time I felt like I wasn't enough, I did what I knew best: I put my head down and worked harder, like the good girl I'd been taught to be.

"She is a good girl," my teachers said. "She always follows directions."

"She is a good girl," my coaches said. "She always works so hard."

"She is a good girl," my parents said. "She always finishes her homework."

"Good girl" was a coveted compliment, a clear acknowledgment of my value, and its repeated emphasis throughout my life confirmed that a "good girl" was the most desirable thing to be.

As I learned to rely upon the voices of authority figures around me, their approval became an anchor of my self-worth, and my success a reflection of theirs. When I did well, every "good girl" brought with it a temporary high. But that moment quickly dissipated as their attention moved elsewhere, as it inevitably does, leaving me grasping for the next accomplishment that could give me my next hit of validation. When I received praise for meeting expectations, I felt relief—I was the good girl they wanted me to be—but when I didn't—An A- instead of an A+, a silver medal instead of gold—the oppressive weight of their disappointment immediately triggered a deep sense of guilt and shame I could never seem to shake off. The result of this Pavlovian response was that I developed the belief that my value hinged upon my achievements and my ability to please others. I learned to be my teacher's pet, my coach's favorite, my parent's gold-medal-winning, Ivy League–bound daughter . . . but I never learned my own worth.

By the time I graduated college, a shiny Yale degree in hand, I had already landed a yearlong paid fellowship to do research in China, followed immediately by a respectable job at a hedge fund in New York. "Be grateful," I was told. "Very few people receive opportunities like this." So when I first started my career, I nodded along, gratefully accepting the first offer without negotiating, diligently tackling additional assignments without complaint, unquestioningly staying overtime without asking for a raise. I was so busy trying to prove that I was good enough that it never occurred to me that I deserved more.

But as time went on, I started to notice something; no matter how hard I worked or how perfect I tried to be, I was not advancing as quickly as the men around me. Being a good girl had gotten me in the door, but now that I was inside, I had to learn a whole new set of rules, and I was not even close to winning.

Looking back, I wish someone had told me that being a good girl wasn't a prize, *it was a trap*. A deadly trap that came with insurmountable expectations and invisible chains of self-doubt, guilt, and most detrimental of all, *shame*.

Shame is the reason why I didn't push back when my boss underpaid me. Shame is the reason I didn't speak up when my investor blackmailed me. Shame is the reason I settled for a complicit silence, because deep down I didn't believe I was valuable enough.

It took me years to realize that none of it was my fault. I had been brainwashed. Brainwashed to passively accept less. Brainwashed to be stupidly grateful just to have a chance to be in the room. Brainwashed to silently suffer the condescension, the rudeness, the disrespect that every woman is so intimately familiar with.

After a lifetime of small paper cuts—being overlooked, undervalued, undermined, and assumed as inferior—I finally had enough.

I was done staying silent.

I was done waiting for permission.

I was done being a good girl.

I *chose* to become a Bad Bitch.

I *chose* to unapologetically create life on my own terms.

Now, you also have a choice.

You can passively let life happen to you as a good girl, accepting the meager scraps left over from the men at the top, or you can choose to become a Bad Bitch, and start actively taking your life into your own hands.

In order to do so, you must first understand the ways in which you have been brainwashed. The roots of Good Girl Brainwashing run deep, so it's time to pull them out and undo the damage, so you, too, can unleash your inner Bad Bitch.

THE ROOTS OF GOOD GIRL BRAINWASHING

Why do we criticize our flaws before admiring our strengths?

Why do we fail to negotiate and advocate for our worth?

Why do we downplay our accomplishments?

Why do we stay silent when we know the answer?

Why do we feel shame expressing our needs and boundaries?

And why is it that no matter how hard we work, how qualified we are, or how successful we become, we still never seem to be valued as much as the man next to us, even, or especially, if he is less qualified?

Women today are more ambitious and educated than ever. In the US, women now hold 60 percent of all undergraduate and graduate degrees and are starting businesses at five times the national average. Globally, women account for 47 percent of the workforce and control more than $31 trillion in annual spending. On the surface, women now have almost all the same opportunities as men: the ability to own property, open bank accounts, start businesses, sit on boards, and lead corporations—options that weren't even conceivable just a few decades ago. But despite these strides, despite public lip service paid to female empowerment initiatives, women continue to get paid less, promoted less, and invested in less than our male counterparts, while still being expected to do more . . . Why?

Because we have yet to address the insidious root of the problem: Good Girl Brainwashing.

Good Girl Brainwashing is a set of subconscious messages perpetuated by society and media that train women to stay silent, small, and subordinate. It teaches us that in order to be accepted by the status quo, we must shrink ourselves for the sake of others, to ask permission before taking up space, and to seek validation before taking action. We learn to doubt our dreams and question the validity of even having them in the first place.

An insidious long-term epidemic, Good Girl Brainwashing has flown under the radar for centuries with symptoms including low self-worth, people-pleasing, perfectionism, imposter syndrome, and weak boundaries. If left untreated, these symptoms easily escalate into more serious maladies: burnout, depression, and even suicide. Since Good Girl Brainwashing has never officially been classified as a disease, a woman is quickly dismissed as ludicrous if she ever dares to bring up her symptoms seriously. How many times has a woman been called "crazy" for simply asking for an equal voice in a decision? How many times has she been called "overdramatic" for simply asking for a safe space to work? This phenomenon is called "gaslighting"—using psychological manipulation to cause someone to question their own sanity—and it's exactly how our patriarchal culture has kept women quiet, obedient, and confused throughout history. It's a tale as old as time.

The most celebrated Western philosophers literally described women as incomplete men: Aristotle said, "The female is female by virtue of a lack of certain qualities. We should regard women's nature as suffering from natural defectiveness."

The Bible labeled a woman as an incidental being subject to the whim of man's ego: Eve was born from Adam's rib for the primary purpose of keeping him company, so he wouldn't get lonely.

America's Founding Fathers destroyed centuries-long Native American matrilineal traditions that viewed women as the sacred life-givers and landowners: the colonizers usurped this custom and gave men sole claim to life, liberty, and property.

Early Western psychology cemented a woman's psychosexual inadequacy: Sigmund Freud, the founder of psychoanalysis, coined the popular term "penis envy" to describe a young girl's anxiety and inferiority upon the realization she does not have a penis.

These narratives have brainwashed us to blindly accept the most toxic lie of all . . . that women are weak, inferior, and never enough.

Today, this lie continues to be perpetuated by media messages that tell us from an early age:

You are not pretty enough

You are not skinny enough

You are not smart enough

You are not brave enough

You are not experienced enough

While we cannot tangibly hear or see the brainwashing, its insidious impact compounds over our lifetimes.

We ask, "What if I get the answer wrong?" and don't raise our hands.

We ask, "What if I don't have the right qualifications?" and don't apply for the job.

We ask, "What if he thinks I'm too pushy?" and don't assert our boundaries.

We ask, "What if they think I'm selfish?" and never take time for ourselves.

We're so brainwashed into believing that we need to be perfect, that we need to be liked, that we hand our power over on a silver platter to anyone and everyone but ourselves.

Here's the thing, the patterns that may have served us as good girls become severe detriments to us as women. Good girl behavior—obedience, politeness, self-effacing modesty, perfectionism—becomes:

- Not speaking up
- Not asking for help
- Not advocating for our worth
- Not asserting our boundaries
- Not sharing our needs
- Not negotiating our pay
- And settling for *way less* than we deserve

Without consciously realizing it, every seemingly small, insignificant moment of repressed silence slices away a piece of our personal power. Repeated enough times, these moments deepen into scars, creating cycles of self-limiting beliefs and self-sabotaging behavior that become harder and harder to break. When we accept that our voices are somehow secondary to those around us, we begin to believe:

It is best to remain silent about our needs, wants, and desires.

It is best to keep our opinions and questions to ourselves.

It is best to diminish ourselves and stay small for the sake of others' comfort.

But at some point, no matter how hard it is, we must choose to break free of these vicious cycles. Every good girl, in her evolution to becoming a Bad Bitch, has one thing in common: SHE WAKES THE FUCK UP. She *chooses* to become aware of the self-sacrificing patterns and the oppressive narratives that are no longer serving her, and she *chooses* to break free of them once and for all.

Once I chose to become a Bad Bitch, I discovered that the most powerful thing I could do was bet on myself. I bet on myself when I quit my stable corporate finance job, even though my family and friends thought I was crazy. I bet on myself when I launched my first startup, even though I had no idea how to incorporate a business. I bet on myself when I decided to raise a venture capital fund, even though there were hardly any women in the industry. Every step of the way, it was my conviction in myself and my own abilities that drove me forward. It was my inner Bad Bitch voice that told me to never settle, to keep going no matter how hard it felt in that moment . . . and I'm so grateful I listened. Today, I'm a four-time USA National Champion and USA Hall of Fame gymnast turned serial entrepreneur, venture capitalist, global public speaker, podcast host, and executive coach. I'm the founder of the Bad Bitch Empire, a global platform building unapologetic worth and wealth for women. I've helped female entrepreneurs raise millions in funding and coached thousands of women to take charge of their careers and grow their businesses, and I am one of the few women of color to successfully raise a fund focused on investing in women-led companies. No one would ever guess that once upon a time I was an awkward, introverted immigrant good girl from the Midwest who always felt like she was never enough.

Now I've made it my mission to help women around the world break free of Good Girl Brainwashing so you, too, can unapologetically turn your Bad Bitch Dreams into reality. If you've picked up this book, you've probably struggled with symptoms of Good Girl Brainwashing—whether it's low self-worth, people-pleasing, or diminishing yourself in any way. It won't be easy to undo a lifetime of brainwashing, but it will be worth it. Together we will release these good girl habits once and for all so you can reclaim your life and finally unleash your inner Bad Bitch to the world.

UNLEASH YOUR BAD BITCH

The term "bitch"—like many other feminine words in the English language—has been repeatedly stigmatized. We refer to "that bitch" as a snarky, cold, heartless woman. "Stop bitching about it," we say to annoying complainers. "I'm going to make you my bitch," a man snarls when he is prepared to utterly embarrass and dominate his competition.

Seems harmless, right? Wrong. Language has weight. The words we use and the meaning we infuse into them alter our entire perception of reality, and for too long the words we have chosen confine women to a claustrophobic cage of inferiority.

I refuse to accept this bastardization of women—our voices, our bodies, and our being—any longer.

Now as we prepare to reclaim our rightful seat at the head of the table, not only will we reclaim the word "bitch," we will proudly proclaim the superior ways of the Bad Bitch.

Bad Bitch: A woman who unapologetically takes charge of her *body*, her *boundaries*, and her *bank account*. A Bad Bitch knows who she is, knows what she wants, and knows she's going to get it.

Each and every woman has the ability to activate the Bad Bitch that is already inside of her. The Bad Bitch is the woman you could be if you showed up as your most powerful and authentic self. It's the version of you that appears when you've let go of unnecessary fears and feel free to speak your truth and pursue your greatest dreams. The Bad Bitch is courageous, passionate, and abundant, exuding the grace and magnanimity inherent in all truly powerful women. Unlike the good girl who succumbs to external validation and judgments, the Bad Bitch is willing to push the limits regardless of what other people think or say. Unlike the good girl who convinces you that you are not worth the risk, that you'll fail regardless, the Bad Bitch doesn't consider failure an option. She doesn't wait for permission; she simply strikes and never looks back. A Bad Bitch who knows her worth refuses to accept anything less than what she deserves. When someone doesn't appreciate her value, she doesn't lean in and work harder; she leans the fuck back and walks away, because a Bad Bitch always has options.

Being a Bad Bitch is especially crucial in business because to this day, business is still a male-dominated domain. Men occupy over 90 percent of Fortune 500 CEO roles, 75 percent of senior roles, and control over 90 percent of investment capital, which means that the boys' club is still alive and kicking. Why does this matter? Because the boys' club is where decisions get made—who gets promoted, who gets investment, and who gets access to the most important deals. The previous generations of women fought hard to help us break into this club—setting critical standards for fair pay and antidiscrimination— but the mistake is believing that simply being in the room is enough. The majority of us are still sitting on the sidelines, quietly abiding by boys' club rules, too busy being polite, obeying authority, and doubting our own capabilities to recognize how much value we can bring to the table. We have passively accepted the status quo for too long, working hard for mediocre bosses, dealing with disrespect, and staying silent in the face of harassment. We have been brainwashed to believe that men are naturally better at business, that they're smarter with money, and that they have a higher penchant for risk-taking.

Let's call this out for what it is: TOTAL BULLSHIT. As women, we have unique perspectives and skills that are invaluable to the future of business, and we've worked too hard for too long to not start earning the money, power, and respect we deserve.

On behalf of all Bad Bitches, I say: *Enough is enough.*

From this point on, let's make it clear that we are *done.*

Done with being pleasant.

Done with people-pleasing.

Done with silencing our voices.

Done with blindly following orders.

Done with living below our potential.

Done with working for other people's dreams.

It is time to put yourself FIRST.

Being a Bad Bitch means having the courage to bet on your own dreams, because if you don't bet on yourself, no one else will. It means advocating for yourself, asserting your values, and calling out bullshit, even if other people call you "difficult" or "crazy." Because if you're making moves and busting the status quo, you *will* have haters, you *will* be told to stand down, you *will* get rejected, you *will* be called names. But guess what? None of that matters. Your opinion of yourself is the most important one. So long as you've got your own back and you are staying true to yourself, the right people and opportunities *will* come your way. A good girl inevitably hits a ceiling in her career. A Bad Bitch says, "What ceiling?"

Now, if you've spent your whole life as a good girl following rules and still aren't fully convinced, I'll give it to you straight. Being a good girl might get you a pat on the head, but it will never get you respect or power. Without respect or power, you are stuck in good girl purgatory. If you want to rise up, understand that the best business leaders don't do business with those who are "nice," we do business with those we respect, and we respect people who have confidence in what they bring to the table. We respect people with integrity, boundaries, and unwavering values. We respect people who can lead us forward, confront challenges, and communicate directly, even when it's uncomfortable. At the end of the day, the good girl gets the coffee, the Bad Bitch gets the bag. There's a big difference.

So if you are ready to become a Bad Bitch, you need to fully *commit* to being a Bad Bitch. That means committing to pushing yourself outside of your comfort zone and believing in yourself so much that it hurts. It means you need to stop giving a fuck about what other people think about you. Stop caring about being liked. Bad Bitches don't care about being liked; we want to be respected. Respect brings money, money brings power, and power gives us the ability to create our Bad Bitch Empires.

Most importantly, being a Bad Bitch means you commit to *never settle*.

Never settle even though it might feel easier.

Never settle even though that's the way "things have always been."

Never settle even when people try to break you down.

Settling is the hallmark of a good girl, but a Bad Bitch cannot afford to settle.

We are at a critical inflection point in history. Women now control 32 percent of the world's wealth, and this will rise to a staggering $97 trillion by 2024. By the end of the decade, there will be an unprecedented shift in economic power as women in the US are expected to take control of two-thirds of all US wealth—that's an additional $30 trillion transferring into the hands of women in America alone. As traditional institutions, economic systems, and power structures are being overturned, Bad Bitches like us can finally rise and reclaim our power.

What are you waiting for?

We've come this far because the Bad Bitches before us were unwilling to settle. The only way we will continue to make strides toward the collaborative and diverse future we want to see is if we all refuse to settle.

It's our turn now.

YOUR BODY. YOUR BOUNDARIES. YOUR BANK ACCOUNT.

The Bad Bitch Business Bible will serve as an invaluable guide as you ascend the business world. These are the lessons no one will ever teach you in school. These are the lessons that I and other successful Bad Bitches have learned, often the hard way, to succeed in the male-dominated business world. In this bible I'll be sharing real stories from my naive good girl days, and the no-nonsense Bad Bitch tips and tactics I wish someone had shared with me a long time ago. Not only would it have saved me a lot of pain, it would have made me a lot more money.

The ten Bad Bitch Commandments are divided into three parts to help you take charge of your: 1) Body; 2) Boundaries; 3) Bank Account.

1. **BODY:** What does your body have to do with succeeding in business? Everything. As women, we have been continually shamed for our bodies, and this shame runs deep. Shame affects our confidence in ourselves, our abilities, and our power. When we are ashamed of the woman we see in the mirror, it's impossible to rise to our full potential. To become Bad Bitches in business, we must unapologetically bring our whole authentic selves to the table, and that requires that we first learn to love, respect, and believe in ourselves. Taking charge of your body like a Bad Bitch means letting go of shame, owning your voice, and never apologizing for taking up space. Once you commit to being a Bad Bitch, you'll discover that the power you needed was always inside of you. In this section, you'll learn to access your own unique superpowers, speak your truth, define your Bad Bitch Dream, and show up with the Bad Bitch Energy required to turn those dreams into a reality.

2. **BOUNDARIES:** People-pleasing, saying "yes" when you want to say "no," allowing subpar behavior . . . sound familiar? In this section, we'll talk about how to say "no" to toxic people, work, and environments that do not serve your higher self. You'll learn how to own your wins, call out bullshit, and set strong boundaries so you can prioritize yourself and protect your dreams. Boundaries allow you to focus on the work that matters to you and rise above the noise that doesn't. Don't worry, setting strong boundaries doesn't mean you're isolating yourself and doing it alone. In fact, it's the opposite. When you have strong boundaries, you create room for the right people to join your team—the ones who add value to your life, rather than drain it. You gain the capacity to evaluate who truly deserves to be in your life, and you start rolling with winners. That's how a Bad Bitch stays on top.

3. **BANK ACCOUNT:** Once you've invested in building up your body and your boundaries, it's time to translate that value into actual dollars and cents in your bank account. In this section, you'll learn

how to finally command your worth so you can negotiate, earn, and raise the money you deserve. You'll learn how to stop undervaluing yourself and letting other people dictate your prices. You'll learn how to develop a positive money mindset so you can start making money work for you, instead of against you. You'll also discover how to maximize your wealth and impact through the exponential power of investing together with a community of Bad Bitches. At the end of the day, you can't be a full-fledged Bad Bitch until you take charge of your bank account. Money is a tool for freedom to live life on your own terms, and this freedom is exactly what previous generations of women have fought so hard to earn. You start making money like a Bad Bitch the moment you commit to a greater vision for yourself and the world, and refuse to settle for anything less than you're worth. Once you are rolling in Bad Bitch dough, they can try to diminish you, they can try to disrespect you, but you'll be laughing all the way to the bank.

Remember, being a Bad Bitch isn't a destination, it's a way of life. It's a mode of being, acting, and doing that unapologetically presents your value and worth in any interaction you have, any situation you encounter, and any decision you make. Stay firmly rooted as a Bad Bitch, and you will surely attract the right opportunities and people toward you: The ones who see your power, respect it, and support it.

BEFORE WE BEGIN

One last note before you embark on this journey. The most crucial thing to remember about being a Bad Bitch is our shared duty in uplifting other women: every time a Bad Bitch stands up for herself, she is taking a stand for all women. When I first started unleashing my inner Bad Bitch into the world, it quickly became apparent that it was contagious. When I shared my truth and my power with other women, they absorbed it and turned it into their own. As one of my coaching clients said to me, "Seeing you go to the edge gives me permission to take a baby step." This is when I realized that I have a duty to embrace every aspect of myself—to forgive my failures, love my flaws, and speak up for myself and the women around me. I have a duty to take ownership of my evolving story, to be unapologetic in demanding what I deserve, and to share my learnings, because one woman's actions create a ripple effect for all the women around her. **A Bad Bitch embraces her power and gives other women the space and support to do the same.**

The Bad Bitch Business Bible exists to help you gain the respect, money, and power you deserve. No matter what career path you choose to pursue, this bible will give you the mindset and the tools to unapologetically take charge of your body, your boundaries, and your bank account so you can become the Bad Bitch you were born to be. Read the Bad Bitch Commandments, take them to heart, reflect on them regularly, and you will never again forget WHO THE FUCK YOU ARE: a Bad Bitch knows what she wants and gets what she wants, every damn time.

Always remember:

BAD BITCHES NEVER SETTLE.

PART ONE

BODY

"In a world that feeds off your insecurity,
loving yourself is an act of rebellion."

—Lisa Carmen Wang

A BAD BITCH IS UNBREAKABLE

NEVER ENOUGH

My career as a competitive gymnast began when I was nine years old, and with it, a deep-seated drive to be perfect at all costs. As the daughter of immigrants, I understood the impossibly high stakes of failure. As a student, I slaved for straight As, but especially as a national champion gymnast, I mastered the art of perfection. Perfect tens, perfect posture, perfect smile. My perfection seeded within me the pernicious habit of ignoring my body for the sake of more achievement, more acknowledgment, and more approval. When my body was screaming with fatigue, I pushed myself even harder. When I was hungry and agitated, I became even stricter with my diet. When I was injured, I told everyone I was "fine," and got right back on the mat. Perfection does not care about pain.

By the time I was eighteen years old, I had steadily risen in the ranks to become the defending US National Champion gymnast three years running. After winning the gold medal at the Pan American Games in Rio de Janeiro, Brazil, also known as "The Olympics of North and

South America," there was only one more competition to conquer, the World Championships, the qualifier for the ultimate prize: the 2008 Beijing Olympic Games.

When competition day finally arrived, I became acutely aware of how much was on the line. I thought about all that my parents had sacrificed, all the hours my coach had put into me. Ten years of hard work hinged upon this one moment. This one perfect routine.

Hearing my name called and stepping onto the mat, I felt the mounting pressure of the country's expectations and an overwhelming fear of failure creeping up on me. I smiled with all the confidence I could muster, walked to the corner of the mat, and settled into my beginning pose. The music began, and I leapt into my first moves: back walkover, side split, balance, pose, sashay, toss, turning split jump . . . Normally, I'd allow muscle memory to take over and feel the flow of my body in sync with the rhythm, but this time, as the music crescendoed, so too did the volume of expectations in my head. I became hyperaware of the piercing gazes of the judges, the faces in the crowd, and the pressure to achieve a decade-long dream.

They say all it takes is a flash of doubt, and on that day, doubt determined my fate.

Despite being the National Champion for three years in a row, when it came time to qualify for my Olympic dream . . . I stumbled. I failed to qualify for the Olympic Games by a mere 0.25 tenths of a point.

They say it hurts when your dream falls apart, but there's nothing quite like the pain, the regret of unfulfilled potential, when you are so close you can taste it. In that one moment, everything I believed about myself completely shattered. I felt like a complete failure, like nothing I had done over the past ten years mattered. I replayed my mistakes, picking apart my flaws in a never-ending loop in my head, hating myself more with each passing second. *I wasn't prepared enough. I didn't work hard enough. I wasn't strong enough* . . . That is the insidious nature of perfection. Nothing is ever enough.

I had been the perfect girl my entire life, following the rules, obeying authority, getting the right grades, winning the gold medals, and now I could never be the perfect girl again . . . and, oh, what a blessing that turned out to be.

My greatest fear was failing to make the Olympics, failing my family, my coaches, and myself. Then it happened—and it broke me wide open in both the worst and the best possible ways. I've coached thousands of women, and I always tell them, "Your greatest freedom lies on the other side of your greatest fear," because it was precisely in that moment when I came face-to-face with my greatest fear that I heard the first stirrings of my inner Bad Bitch: the one that refused to settle and said, *Fuck this, this is not how my story ends. I will not allow some random judges to determine my future. I will not allow this outcome to break me.*

That same week, I received my acceptance letter to my dream school, Yale University, but enrolling would mean that I would end my gymnastics career right then and there. I had a choice in that moment: I could leave gymnastics on a losing note, allow my failure to eat me up alive, and become a victim to all the voices that had told me, *You are not good enough, strong enough, qualified enough to succeed*, or I could become the main character of my own story and fight for the greatest comeback of my life.

I chose the latter.

While the rest of my peers started college, I made the extremely difficult decision to defer enrollment to Yale, and instead committed to one more year of the most grueling training in order to become the best gymnast I could be. Even after I made the decision, there were plenty of people who told me to just quit, and there were countless moments when I also questioned my choice. But in the end, I knew it was the only option. I had to rewrite my story, and this time I wasn't doing it for anyone else: I was doing it for me. I bought a one-way ticket to the Russian Olympic Training center to train with the toughest coaches in the world, and spent the next nine months tirelessly training, traveling, and competing across Europe. For the first time in my career, I was liberated from the fear of failure and the fear of being imperfect. Now I was just hungry to win, on my own terms.

A year later, I arrived at my final competition, the USA National Championships, with the hard-earned confidence of a Bad Bitch who had rebuilt herself from the inside out. I had visualized this competition for an entire year, and I would not settle for anything less than gold. In the end, I finished that competition and my athletic career exactly how I wanted: with an undefeated gold sweep—winning every single gold medal and being crowned Athlete of the Year. I proved to everyone, and most importantly, to myself, that I was more than enough.

As I stood on the highest podium one last time, I remembered all the times I had fallen, all the pain I had endured, all the humiliation I had felt when my Olympic dream was shattered, and I realized that I had gained something even more valuable than the medals and the recognition: I had gained, bit by painstaking bit, an unshakeable confidence in my own ability to fall and get back up again. They say good girls are fragile. But I was not a good girl anymore.

I was unbreakable.

PERFECT IS THE OPPOSITE OF POWERFUL

Growing up, we are rarely told that we are powerful. In fact, we're usually told the opposite, that we're weak, that we must be careful, that we cannot protect ourselves. As society molds us to become obedient, hardworking good girls adhering to an impossible standard of perfection, it also trains us to be fearful of failure, of judgment, of being a disappointment. So instead of going for big, audacious goals, we spend all our energy trying to please others. Instead of jumping in boldly, we opt out of the game and claim we are losers before we've even had a chance to make the first move. Perfectionism is toxic precisely because it prevents us from trying. Trained to constantly see failure instead of opportunity, there's a part of us that's always waiting for someone else's permission and asking, "Do you think I'm ready?" Instead of asking, "How high, how fast, and when do I start?"

Let's reframe the idea of "failure." Most people, especially perfectionists, tend to think of failure as a binary: Pass or fail. Nothing in between. In this zero-sum mindset, if you ask for something and you get rejected, you are a failure. If you launch your project and it doesn't gain as much momentum as you expected, you are a failure. So rather than ask for the role you want, rather than start your business today, you decide it's safer to wait, to research, to prepare, to perfect every last detail, to make sure you have multiple contingency plans ready *just in case* something goes wrong. You convince yourself that you're being diligent and responsible, only to realize a year later that nothing has changed. You're still in the same role, you still haven't launched your project, and deep down you're kicking yourself because you see other people surpassing you. Is it because they are smarter? Stronger? Superior? Unlikely. The only reason less competent people are moving ahead of you is because they didn't hesitate. They didn't get stuck in fear. They got in the game and started playing while you were sitting on the sidelines doubting yourself. If you find yourself in the mode where you're always "getting ready"— maybe you've spent months, or years, working on your side project or pitch deck, gathering "feedback" from others, or waiting for the "perfect moment"—let me break it to you: There is no such thing as the perfect moment. You will never feel 100 percent ready. In fact, the longer you stall, the more your fears will start to creep in:

"What if I fail?"

"What if I'm rejected?"

"What if I'm crazy?"

"What if I'm wrong?"

"What if I disappoint them?"

"What if I'm not enough?"

These are your fearful good girl voices that have been trained to "catastrophize"—in other words, projecting all the ways in which things can go wrong. Catastrophizing is something good girls are brainwashed to do, but most of the time it goes unnoticed because it is hidden under the guise of being careful or prepared. "Thorough." You might convince yourself that your dreams are "too risky," or comfort yourself that you're "just being rational," but really, it's your ego's way of protecting itself.

As women, we tend to be significantly more self-critical and more likely to blame ourselves, especially when things don't go according to plan. But when something goes right, we credit circumstance—or other people—for our success. Why does this matter? Because there are real career consequences to this pattern of behavior. While we are preoccupied with overthinking all the ways we might make a wrong move, men are on the other side making money.

What's a Bad Bitch to do? It might feel counterintuitive, but to achieve growth and success, we must release the need to be perfect. Trying to be perfect is not only unhelpful, it is actively harming us. Perfection keeps us in an almost-permanent state of indecision, falsely believing that our power lies outside of us, rather than within us. When we try to be perfect, we give our power away to others because we are waiting for someone else's permission to act on our dreams. Perfectionism keeps us too stressed and too obsessed with our short-comings to realize how powerful we already are. You do not have to be perfect to be powerful. In fact, perfect is the *opposite* of powerful.

Releasing the need to be perfect liberated me in the final year of my gymnastics career because it was the first time I stopped seeking permission. I took the leap to defer college, to go to a foreign country, to train with the toughest coaches in the world even though there was no guarantee anything would work out. But it was that independent choice that helped me discover the inner strength that I carried into my professional career. I discovered that it's okay to leap even when you don't have a perfect plan. It's okay to choose a different direction even when you don't know exactly where it's going to lead. It's okay to bet on yourself even when no one else will bet on you. What I really learned was that I could *trust myself* to have my own back. When I quit my cushy finance job to become an entrepreneur, I *trusted* that I would be able to figure out how to make my own money. When I almost lost everything due to a toxic business partner, I *trusted* that I would eventually build an even bigger empire. I knew that no matter what happened, I would not only survive, I would thrive. I proved to *myself* that I was unbreakable, and that is a superpower no one can ever take away from me.

YOUR CRACKS GIVE YOU CHARACTER

Being unbreakable is not just being resilient. Consider a vase: when it breaks, it shatters into hundreds, if not thousands, of pieces. Any attempt to put it back together results in a version worse than the original. To be resilient is like a tough rubber band. Even if it stretches, it bounces back to its original form; however, to be unbreakable is to grow stronger from any kind of stress, pressure, or crack. Something that is unbreakable, changes form, and evolves into something more magnificent than it originally was.

Kintsugi, which translates to "golden joinery," is the Japanese art of taking cracked pottery and mending the broken areas with gold, silver, or platinum lacquer. As a philosophy, *kintsugi* embraces and celebrates imperfections. Cracks are a symbol of life's inevitable chaos and the beauty of rebirth in the wake of destruction. Not only is there no attempt to hide the damage, but the cracks are literally illuminated.

Like *kintsugi* art, what makes people interesting and complex isn't their successes, but the failures they overcome on their journey to success. No Bad Bitch is successful because everything was easy. In fact, it's usually the opposite. The Baddest Bitches I know are the ones who took the risk to go after a big, bold dream and, despite encountering failure many times over, chose to get right back up and keep moving forward. So the next time fear gets in your way, remind yourself: your cracks give you character. I'd go as far as to say that Bad Bitches *live* for the cracks. Any dream worth fighting for will be filled with inevitable rejection, criticism, and pain. You must see obstacles not only as something to overcome, but as opportunities to learn, grow, and celebrate. A Bad Bitch is unbreakable; therefore, any obstacle is an opportunity.

BAD BITCH REPLAY

"There's no one I can say these awful words out loud to, who won't judge or make me hate myself more than I already do. Except you." This was the ominous opening line of an email I received from Serena months after our coaching program had ended. Serena went on to describe how she had spent the last year courting an investor for the $1 million in funding she needed to grow her company. The investor had continued stringing her along, promising he would wire the money, but would always find a last-minute excuse not to. In the meantime, Serena started dipping into her own savings to hire her team and build out her technology, believing she would soon be reimbursed by the investor's funding. However, months later, the investor suddenly backed out with no explanation, and Serena was left with nothing. After years of meticulously growing her savings, she barely had a dime left in her bank account and now had to choose between paying her own bills or paying her team. She was in the hardest financial position of her life and nearing her breaking point.

When we got together for an emergency coaching session, she shared the full story through tears, crying about the investor's betrayal. "I can't believe he screwed me over like that! What kind of person does that? I'll never recover from this. I'm ruined . . ." She was rapidly spiraling into the good girl trap of blame and victimhood, rather than taking ownership of the situation. We had to get her out of the victim mentality and back into Bad Bitch mode.

The first step in getting Serena back on track was to have her recommit to the Radical Self-Responsibility Pledge. It goes: "I take radical self-responsibility for my thoughts, feelings, and actions—under no circumstances will I blame others. I am the author of my own story. I am the master of my own reality." Every coaching client I work with takes this pledge, because accepting full responsibility for your choices is a declaration of your power. When you take the Radical Self-Responsibility Pledge, you commit to being an unbreakable Bad Bitch who's in charge of your own destiny, rather than the victim of circumstances that are beyond your control. As a victim, you ask, "Why is this happening to me?" As a Bad Bitch, you ask, "What am I going to do about it?"

For many people, accepting and practicing Radical Self-Responsibility is daunting; it's much easier to blame other people and circumstances outside your control. While it may be true that the world is unfair, people are mean, or the economy sucks, you always have the power to decide how you will respond to the situation in front of you. Especially when difficult situations arise, Radical Self-Responsibility empowers you to rise above external events and reclaim your own agency in shaping what you want to happen in the moment and going forward.

Once Serena had recommitted to the Radical Self-Responsibility Pledge, the next step was to reframe her perceived failure as an opportunity for growth. She needed to remember that no matter how terrible or unfair the current situation was, she was not a helpless good girl—she was a Bad Bitch who had risen from challenges many times before and could (and would) do so again.

It was time for her Bad Bitch Replay.

What Is the Bad Bitch Replay?

It's a simple but powerful exercise in which you replay a memory of a past failure, except rather than focusing on all the ways you failed, you focus on all the ways you grew. As you go through the replay, describe how you used your superpowers to turn your failure around and how you became an unbreakable Bad Bitch. In effect, you are rewriting your story so you can focus on your own power and agency, rather than being at the mercy of external circumstances. There are three important rules to keep in mind to create a powerful Bad Bitch Replay:

1. **BECOME THE NARRATOR:** Instead of describing yourself in the first person using "I/me," when writing your Bad Bitch Replay, affirm yourself in the third-person perspective with "she/her" or "they/them" pronouns (or however else you'd like to identify). By narrating your story in the third person, you are activating the power of metacognition—in other words, stepping back to objectively observe your current situation and becoming aware of your automatic reactions and thoughts. Metacognition is a powerful tool I use to create distance from my current emotions and environment so I can determine the best next steps to take. Think of it as creating an out-of-body experience, like watching yourself as the protagonist in a movie you wrote and directed. For example, instead of saying, "The investors shit on my presentation, and now I'll never get funded," you might say, "Lea pitched her new startup. While

she didn't get funding, she received helpful feedback that she'll incorporate for her next pitch."

2. **STAY POSITIVE AND AFFIRMATIVE:** As you tell your story, avoid the urge to focus on weaknesses or criticizing mistakes. Instead, focus on building your Bad Bitch up: What do you admire about her work ethic, creativity, or bravery? In what ways is she a role model? Take note of areas where you haven't given yourself the credit you deserve and praise your positive traits. For example, "Jessica is brave for putting her ideas out into the world. She works incredibly hard and will find investors who will fund her dream no matter what it takes."

3. **BE ACTION-ORIENTED:** Describe the steps this Bad Bitch took afterward to turn the negative event into a positive one. Remember, whereas a victim passively complains about events that happen *to* her, a Bad Bitch takes an active role to make any situation work *for* her. Ask yourself, what superpowers did she activate to overcome this challenging moment? What lessons did she learn? How does she become even stronger from this experience?

When Serena first described her situation, her story was, "This investor screwed me over, I lost all my money, and I don't know how I'll ever be able to pay myself and my team." Even if all this was true, by being negative and passive, she would stay stuck in victim mode feeling sorry for herself. In contrast, when I asked her to replay the story of herself as a Bad Bitch, she shared, "Serena believed wholeheartedly in the vision for her company. Her passion attracted both teammates and investors to support her. While the investment fell through, she wasn't willing to give up. She was resourceful and reached out to her community for support, she redid her business model, she learned from her mistakes, and she knows better for next time to trust her gut and communicate directly if anything feels off."

I asked her to describe her superpowers: "Serena always sees the best in people and situations. People trust her because she cares. She's committed to her team and making sure everyone around her succeeds—that is her superpower."

Finally, I asked her, "Why is Serena unbreakable?" She replied, "Serena is unbreakable because she never gives up, and she's not about to start now. She grew up in a household that was always strapped for cash. While her mom was working two jobs to support the family, Serena had to take care of her siblings. She never had a single penny handed to her, but no matter how bad things got, she always stayed optimistic. That optimism has gotten her through tough times. So even though this investment didn't go the way she wanted it to, she knows it's not the end. Her vision is way too strong to break, and so is she."

Her eyes lit up as she spoke, the words breathing her power back into her. Her Bad Bitch Replay gave us irrefutable evidence: She was not a fragile good girl. She'd never been. She was an unbreakable Bad Bitch who would find a way, just like she always had, to turn things around. Serena recommitted herself to rebuilding her business from the ground up, and after a year of tireless work, she successfully secured a $1.5 million investment, this time from investors who fully understood and aligned with her vision.

Your Bad Bitch Replay

When I wrote out my Bad Bitch Replay, I made myself relive that dream-shattering moment of missing the Olympics. As much as my perfectionist self wanted to focus on what I could have done better, I trained my mind to let go of the mistakes and the eventual outcome. Instead, I focused on who I had become in the process: a fighter, a winner, and an unbreakable Bad Bitch that never gives up. I discovered my superpowers are my ability to stay positive, to act bravely and boldly, and to inspire others to do the same. Every time I feel down, I remind myself, *If I can pick myself up from that moment, I can pick myself up from anything.*

Now it's your turn to write your Bad Bitch Replay. Think about a low point in your life when you experienced significant adversity or failure—perhaps you made a devastating mistake, a bad decision, or just a total fool of yourself—then think about how you turned (or will turn) that moment around into an opportunity. Use the following prompts to guide you: the goal is to paint a picture of yourself as an unbreakable Bad Bitch who you deeply admire and trust to overcome any tough situation.

This Bad Bitch's name is _____

Her best friends would describe her as . . .

_____

_____

A low point in her life/a time she failed was when . . .

_____

_____

She picked herself up from that moment by . . .

_____

_____

She discovered her superpowers are . . .

_____

_____

She learned valuable lessons, including . . .

_____

_____

She is a role model and inspiration to others because . . .

_____

_____

She is an unbreakable Bad Bitch because . . .

_____

_____

How does it feel to describe yourself as a Bad Bitch? Does this sound like someone you admire and respect? If not, keep writing until you can own your superpowers like the Bad Bitch you are.

This is a crucial exercise. A lot of women spend far too much time criticizing themselves, and all this does is set us up to fail. Why? Because your thoughts dictate your feelings, your feelings dictate your actions, and your actions dictate your outcomes. If you're viewing yourself as an imperfect, failing human that will never be good enough, do you think you're more likely to succeed or fail?

By committing to your Bad Bitch Replay and staying positive and affirmative, you are taking charge of your own internal narrative. By changing how you think of yourself, you'll change how you feel and how you act, and be far more likely to bring about your desired outcomes. Remember, Bad Bitches don't spend time feeling sorry for themselves. We learn, grow, and keep moving forward.

YOUR BAD BITCH DREAM

When I look back at my early career, the only regret I have is not betting on myself sooner—that includes doubting myself, working for leaders I didn't respect, and putting other people's dreams above my own. The reason I did those things? Because deep down, I still didn't believe I was worthy. I was afraid to state what I really wanted: a career I was passionate about, surrounded by a team I respected and admired, waking up every morning excited to make a big impact, with the creative freedom to work on my own terms. I vividly remember slogging through my first corporate finance job, afraid to even consider the possibility of being an entrepreneur because the thought of it was simply too risky, too undefined, especially for a good girl who was new to the business game. How did I eventually build the confidence to take the leap? I started by defining and visualizing my Bad Bitch Dream.

Your Bad Bitch Dream is the big dream you would pursue if you stopped asking, "What if everything goes *wrong*?" and started asking, "What if everything goes *right*?" It's a subtle shift, but an extremely powerful one. Your Bad Bitch Dream is your heart's deepest desire, something you've always wanted but secretly have been afraid to admit because the dream feels too big, too bold, too crazy. You don't speak it into existence because a part of you thinks, *Who am I to do this?* But think about it: If you're too afraid to even admit to yourself what you want, how will you ever get what you want?

Want to know my Bad Bitch Dream? As an Asian American woman, I grew up never seeing myself in the media, feeling worthless, ugly, and invisible. So deep down, I dreamed of building a global platform that could amplify diverse women who were missing from mainstream cultural conversations. I wanted to be a role model, media personality, and public speaker who could help women feel powerful, beautiful, and seen; however, for a long time I was too afraid to put myself out there because I believed I should be "more practical." I also made excuses like "I'm naturally shy," or "I don't have enough experience yet," but really those were just excuses to not face my biggest fears— fear of failure, fear of judgment, fear of not being enough. The problem was, every day that I didn't go after my dream, a little part of me died inside. I knew I wasn't being true to myself, and I knew that I would never reach my full potential if I didn't give my dream a fair shot. So I asked myself, *What if everything goes right?* and reminded myself that if I was capable of boldly stating and acting on my Olympic dream when I was nine years old, then there was nothing preventing me as a grown woman from boldly taking action toward my Bad Bitch Dream. This book that you are holding in your hands is a manifestation of my belief in myself, my mission, and my superpowers. If I can do it, so can you. It's time to get clear on your Bad Bitch Dream.

Bad Bitch Dream Instructions

1. **GET HONEST WITH YOURSELF:** Are you leading a career and life that's fully aligned with your desires? Are you excited to wake up and do the work that's in front of you? Are you giving it your all

and making the most of your superpowers? If you didn't respond with an unequivocal yes, don't worry, you're not alone. Ninety-three percent of Americans state they are not pursuing their dream career; however, just because others are unclear or unintentional, doesn't mean you have to be. Start by being honest and specific about what you want to change about your current reality. This is your chance to lay all your cards out on the table and consider if your current path is the one that you want to continue going down or if something needs to change.

2. **TAP INTO JOY AND ANGER:** It's possible that admitting you want change feels uncomfortable, intimidating, even confusing. Maybe you want to pivot your career but don't know what else to pursue, or maybe all you know is that you're not 100 percent happy with what you're doing, but have no idea which direction to go in. That's okay—I never said this was going to be easy. Sometimes the hardest part of this process is figuring out what you want in the first place. If you're unclear about the direction of your Bad Bitch Dream, there are two primary emotions you can tap into to help clarify things:

Joy

The best and most sustainable kind of work is work you enjoy doing. Your Bad Bitch Dream should be aligned with the activities and experiences that bring you joy. Here are two ways to experience more of it:

- **Create a weekly joy journal:** Look back at the past week and write down all the moments that brought you joy. Was it when you challenged yourself to solve a difficult problem? Or when you were able to help a friend? Or when you got in the flow of a creative exercise? The simplest things can bring joy, and by noticing them, you'll get hints about the types of experiences you want to optimize for in your Bad Bitch Dream.

- **Think back to your childhood:** What did you love to do before the world told you to be practical? When did you feel the freest? Did you get lost in painting? Did you spend hours outside exploring? Did you love acting or sports? Did you nerd out on certain games or books? Did you daydream about traveling to a different time or place? There is no right or wrong answer to any of these questions—the point is to allow yourself to luxuriate in the memories and to find a spark of joy. Follow that spark, and let it grow brighter. Pick up your paints, jump on a bike, go explore, read, play, indulge, and get lost in the thing that makes you feel most alive. It is in this childlike state of joy that you are most likely to discover a dream that is aligned with our most authentic self.

Anger

Just as joy can make you feel alive, a counterintuitive emotion you can follow is anger. Anger is the first spark of passion; it's a great indicator of what you care most about solving and can point you in the direction of your greater purpose.

- **Ask yourself, *When was the last time I was really angry?*:** Think back to a time or circumstance that really upset you. What happened? Who was involved? Did someone do or say something that was disrespectful or inappropriate? Were you dealing with a sexist or racist asshole? Was it a nasty breakup with a toxic ex? Were you fighting a troll on social media? Was there something on the news that really riled you up?
- **Follow your anger:** Detail the exact moment your anger was triggered, and the events that transpired. Why did you feel so angry? How did the situation aggravate your core values? Who or what made you angry? Who else did it hurt besides you? If you had all the resources and power in the world, what would

you change about the situation so it never happened again? Anger is a powerful source of inspiration for the impact you want to make in the world.

The best long-term career motivators are a combination of joy (the things you love doing) and anger (the problems you feel an emotional drive to solve). Use these emotional sparks to guide your thought process of formulating your Bad Bitch Dream.

1. WRITE OUT YOUR BAD BITCH DREAM BELOW: Remember, a Bad Bitch Dream starts from the foundation of limitless possibility and imagines, *What if everything goes right?* So ask yourself, what career or goal would you pursue now if you couldn't fail? What passion would you pursue if money didn't matter? How big of an impact do you want to make? Be as ambitious as you can. No dream is too big, and the more clearly you define exactly what you want, the more likely you are to get it.

My Bad Bitch Dream is to . . .

_____

My Bad Bitch Dream is worth pursuing because . . . (What impact will it make on yourself and others?)

_____

I am capable of achieving my Bad Bitch Dream because . . .

_____

2. VISUALIZE YOUR BAD BITCH DREAM: Visualization is one of the most powerful mental tools I used throughout my athletic and professional careers. During visualization, you paint a vivid mental picture of your desired state, associating feelings, thoughts, and physical details so that by the time you finish, the future reality that you desire already feels present and tangible. While top-tier athletes invoke the power of visualization to nail a goal, land the flip, or win a game, you can use it to get clear on your Bad Bitch Dream.

To start, close your eyes and fast-forward to the future exactly one year from now. The reason we focus on one year is because it gives us a long enough time frame to work toward creating true change, while also being short enough to create urgency to begin making moves toward your Bad Bitch Dream. Use the following questions to guide you as you visualize yourself going through your dream workday in as much detail as possible. (Approximate time: 10 minutes.)

In my Bad Bitch Dream, my future self . . .
- Begins her day with her dream morning routine . . .
    - How does she energize herself for her day?
    - What does she eat or drink to nourish herself?
    - What does she see when she checks her calendar?

- As she starts her dream workday . . .
    - What kind of work is she doing?
    - What does her dream workspace look like?
    - What kinds of people/team is she surrounded by?

- During the day, she is closing checks and making bank . . .
    - What milestones is she achieving?
    - Who are the dream clients she's working with?
    - How does she feel as she's closing her biggest check to date?

- **And she's feeling good as she's doing it . . .**
  - What is she wearing that makes her feel powerful and confident?
  - How does she walk into the room?
  - What do her colleagues/customers compliment her on?

- **After a successful day at work . . .**
  - What is she proud of herself for?
  - How does she celebrate herself?
  - How does she feel when she looks at her bank account?

- **As she gets ready for bed . . .**
  - What is she grateful for?
  - What rituals does she have to wind down a dream day?
  - What is her last thought before she falls asleep?

What did you see? How did you feel? How is your Bad Bitch Dream different from your current day-to-day reality? Does it seem both ambitious and achievable? Does it make you feel simultaneously nervous and excited? If so, you're on the right track. If not, I invite you to allow yourself to dream even bigger.

Once you've written your Bad Bitch Dream down, the most important thing is to take action. Ask yourself, *What is one thing I can do today that would move me one step closer to my Bad Bitch Dream?* and then commit to doing it ASAP. Every big dream begins with a small step, so don't underestimate it. Even if you don't feel 100 percent sure if your dream is the "right dream" (there's no such thing, by the way), you'll start gathering data about what feels right for you. Remember there is no amount of research or preparation that substitutes for taking action. Your purpose doesn't magically appear; it comes from experimenting, failing, and failing again, until one day something sticks and you decide to commit to it. Moreover, your Bad Bitch Dream will evolve as you do; that's natural. Be patient and recognize that there is no perfect path, only the one that feels the most aligned for you.

Wherever you are on your journey, you can make moves toward your Bad Bitch Dream today. You have so much to offer the world. Focus on what you want and why it matters, and the rest will fall into place; the exact timeline is unimportant. Go ahead, take the leap, and no matter what happens, as an unbreakable Bad Bitch you can always dust yourself off and get right back up again.

COMMANDMENT 2

A BAD BITCH TAKES UP SPACE

SELF-SABOTAGE

"Ew, gross." I blurted out the words in disgust. I was standing in front of the bathroom mirror, glaring at my reflection. A new pimple had just appeared on my forehead, and my lips were unbearably chapped. Never mind that I had just spent eight hours traveling from New York to San Francisco having barely slept the night before—I couldn't cut myself any slack. I stretched the skin under my eyes, trying to artificially tighten the tired bags. Suddenly I noticed a gray hair glistening under the fluorescent bathroom lights, a loathsome weed among my dark locks. The minutes passed as I stood there plucking, pinching, *punishing* myself for my body's perceived imperfections, mesmerized by my own self-loathing.

My phone alarm's blare suddenly jolted me back to reality. I had to get going. I had come to attend my first Silicon Valley networking event and it would be my first time meeting with so many prominent investors and entrepreneurs. I had to make a good first impression.

When I arrived at the event venue, I immediately felt myself shrink.

You don't belong here. Everyone has so much more experience than you. The voice in my head taunted me as I looked around the overwhelming number of men at the networking event. I tried to reverse the self-sabotaging thoughts in real time, reminding myself, *Look confident. You have every right to be here.*

But as a first-time entrepreneur trying to raise money, I couldn't shake off the all-too-familiar feeling that often enveloped me when walking into rooms like this: the feeling of being an outsider, like no matter how hard I tried, I would never fully belong. I knew the odds were against me: female entrepreneurs still received only 2 percent of funding, but I refused to be a victim of bad odds. I was already in the room, after all, so I just needed to figure out how to get the investors to take me, and my little startup, seriously.

I took a few short, jagged breaths holding the air tightly in my chest as I swam cautiously into the sea of men. I was like a minnow among sharks, ready to be eaten alive. I spotted the organizer of the event, an investment partner at a large venture capital fund, and hesitantly approached him. "Um . . . hi," I managed to get out. "Thanks for putting on this great event!" I pasted a big smile on my face in an attempt to look nice and friendly. He looked up from his phone to see who was speaking to him, blinked at me, then continued fiddling with a piece of lint on his Patagonia vest.

I stood there awkwardly, waiting for him to acknowledge me. "Oh!" he said with sudden recognition, "You're Tom's assistant, right?" My face flushed bright red. I had no idea who Tom was, but his flippant dismissal punched the air out of me. Any remaining sliver of confidence completely disappeared. I had felt small before. Now, as I shrank even more into myself, I felt microscopic.

"What? Sorry, I . . . I have my own company," I stammered apologetically, as if I was the one who had made the mistake. But he had already moved on.

That night after the networking event, I stood in front of the bathroom mirror once again, replaying the embarrassing scene that had transpired, berating myself for everything I had done wrong. *Should I have been more assertive? Should I have said something different? Should I have even come here at all?* My thoughts continued down a negative self-sabotage spiral until I had completely beaten myself down. I was utterly exhausted: from the travel, from pushing myself, but more than anything else, from the never-ending self-judgment that I could never seem to escape. As my reflection stared back at me in frustration and dismay, the circles under my eyes noticeably darker, I realized I couldn't keep hitting my breaking point. Something had to change, and that something had to start with how I treated the woman in the mirror.

BODY SHAME IS BAD FOR BUSINESS

Whether in an effort to be pleasing and polite or because we don't feel comfortable in our own skin, Good Girl Brainwashing trains us to diminish and cut ourselves down. Studies show that women have developed a "natural" tendency to assume submissive body language due to centuries of cultural expectations that we must occupy an inferior position to the men around us. Unfortunately, submissive, insecure behavior in women doesn't even seem out of the ordinary. This is Good Girl Brainwashing at its finest: silently poisoning women with the toxic belief that feeling inferior is normal.

When I launched my first podcast, called *Enoughness*, I sought to answer the question "How much is enough?" I didn't understand why, no matter how much I achieved, I never felt like I was good enough. I discovered that while almost everyone experiences a certain degree of "not-enoughness," there is one key difference between how women reacted to the feeling versus men. Society has repeatedly told women that we *are* not enough: not beautiful enough, not skinny enough, not perfect enough. So when a woman doesn't feel like she is enough, she physically shrinks herself. She hunches her shoulders, looks down at the floor, crosses her legs, folds her arms, and takes up as little space as possible so as not to be spotted for her supposed inadequacy.

In contrast, society tells men that they don't *have* enough. They don't have enough money. They don't have enough status. They don't have enough women. The result is populations of men who don't feel like they're enough, but they do the exact opposite of what women do—they physically expand. They take up more space by accumulating more things—more money, more titles, more property, more arm candy—in an effort to prove to the world that they are, in fact, enough. The unfortunate thing about this dichotomy? The business world rewards a man's self-aggrandizing behavior, while it punishes a woman's self-minimizing behavior.

Clearly, learning how to take up space isn't as simple as doing a few power poses. The root of our insecurities runs deep, and it begins at a much more personal level. As a gymnast, I got used to my coaches making offhand remarks like, "Just lose two more pounds, and you'll look acceptable," or "You look fat and ugly in that leotard. Go change." Even if you haven't had this direct experience of someone telling you to your face that your body is unworthy, you are likely not immune to your own version of shame. Shaming our bodies has become so commonplace that we don't even blink an eye when a woman criticizes some physical aspect of herself. In fact, our patriarchal society literally profits off making women feel insecure, ugly, fat, and old. Approximately 91 percent of women are unhappy with their bodies and resort to dieting to achieve their ideal body shape. Fifty-eight percent of college-age girls feel pressured to be a certain weight, and only 5 percent of women naturally possess the body type often portrayed as "ideal" by American media. The average woman spends an average of seventeen years of her life on diets, and tens if not hundreds of thousands of dollars on everything from pills, creams, and surgery to mold themselves to be skinnier, prettier, or younger.

Can you imagine what would happen if one day every single woman woke up and unapologetically loved the Bad Bitch she saw in the mirror? The multi-trillion-dollar makeup, media, and weight-loss industries would crumble overnight.

What does shame have to do with succeeding in business? The answer is: everything. No matter what line of work you are in, no matter what stage of your career you are in, every day you still have to get up and face the same woman in the mirror. How do you speak to that woman? Are you kind to her? Are you grateful for her? Are you appreciative of everything she's done for you? Or are you critical, judgmental, and always trying to find something wrong with her? Self-talk matters. The way we show up for ourselves, especially when no one else is watching, inevitably affects how we show up when they are. If we constantly condemn ourselves in private, how can we possibly expect to be taken seriously in public?

My good girl mistake was getting stuck in shame and obsessing about all the wrong things: the ways my being a woman put me at a disadvantage, the ways other people might judge me as inferior, the ways I was woefully imperfect. I reeked of insecure good girl energy, the kind that invited men to dismiss me as the assistant and shove me into the all-too-common self-shame spiral. How I saw and treated myself directly translated to the way other people saw and treated me, and it finally dawned on me that if I didn't respect myself, others would not respect me. If I didn't see my own power, others would not see it. If I didn't believe myself worthy of taking up space, no one else would believe it, either.

BAD BITCH BODY CHALLENGE

I used to be the kind of woman who rolled her eyes at things like self-love. "I'm busy," I'd say. "I've got things to do, people to meet, goals to achieve—with all of that on my plate, who has time for self-love?" It seemed so soft, so . . . *cringe*. Having grown up defining myself by tangible scores in gymnastics and measurable metrics in business, I bought into the refrain of, "If you can't measure it, you can't manage it." And how in the world do you measure something like self-love?

The answer is, you can't. That's precisely why so few of us, especially the "busy" ones, never make time for it. However, don't let the softness of self-love fool you. The opposite of self-love is self-loathing—a sickness that can kill you from the inside out.

When's the last time you stood in front of the mirror and truly loved the woman you saw? When's the last time you vocalized to her how much you appreciate and respect her? If your answer is anything like mine used to be—some variation of "I don't know . . . never?"— you're not alone, but we're going to fix that right now.

Enter the Bad Bitch Body Challenge, a powerful exercise to help you flip the script of body shame by focusing on the uniqueness, strength, and love that are already within you.

I developed the Bad Bitch Body Challenge after spending years trying to feel good enough by proving myself through external validation and success only to realize that no amount of accolades or money could make me feel better if I didn't love the woman I saw in the mirror. It's a challenge that women of all ages, shapes, colors, and industries have gone through. Participants have ranged from startup founders to corporate employees, from young women just starting their careers to seasoned executives with decades of experience. Every single woman had a different reason for wanting to take the challenge, but the root desire was the same: to release herself from self-sabotaging thoughts and finally feel the power and confidence that had eluded her all her life.

The first step of the Bad Bitch Body Challenge is to get real about the things you say to your body and how you may be sabotaging yourself. Start by standing in front of a full-length mirror . . . naked.

That's right: strip down, stand up, and look yourself straight in the eye. Do a slow body scan from the top of your head all the way down to your toes. What are the critical things you say about your body? What do you wish you could change? In what ways do you think you are not enough? Let the thoughts flow freely and observe them as they appear.

Once you're done with the body scan. Pull out your pen and write down all the negative thoughts that went through your head. Every single little thing. Feel free to use the space below:

_____

_____

_____

_____

Did you get them all? Keep going until you get every last negative thought out.

If this is the first time you're actually seeing your own negativity on paper—all the horrible things you think and say about yourself—you might feel uncomfortable or even appalled. Resist the urge to judge yourself even further. By making your demons visible, you are one step closer to releasing them. Those demons in your head have likely been with you for a long time, but they don't belong to you. They belong to the media, society, your frenemies, or your family, but not to you. Your Bad Bitch self is not petty or hateful; she is powerful and loving, and all you need to do is give yourself a chance to embody her.

Now flip the script to go from self-loathing to self-love. Write down all the things you want to celebrate your body for. You can write things like "I appreciate my body for nourishing me," or "I love how strong my legs are," or "I'm grateful for my health." Write your positive statements down now.

_____

_____

_____

_____

What does it feel like to express gratitude and appreciation to yourself? Was it much harder to find things you love about your body than what you loathe about it?

Here's a confession by one woman who embarked on the Bad Bitch Body Challenge:

I'm not in a place where I can celebrate my body right now. In fact, I'm in a place where in a weak moment, I'm rummaging around for the leftover holiday candy. I've been slowly gaining weight over the last year, and I suspect it's hormonal, which makes me feel it's futile to diet—hence the holiday candy. What the hell?

My body image is not good right now, to say the least. I don't fit into my clothes, so consequently I've only been wearing baggy stuff, which does not make me feel sharp or professional.

I can't even think of one thing I like; that's how disgusted I am. Or is that denial? I am very grateful for my health, of course. But if this is supposed to be honest . . .

Another woman, an athlete turned entrepreneur, shared her experience. You'll see how by simply becoming aware of her thoughts, she was able to make an immediate breakthrough:

Doing these exercises have made me realize that I still carry around much of my self-hate with me. I always want to lose 2–5 pounds, I wish my legs were more elegant, I'm watching the stress take its toll on my face and my hair, and I'm constantly obsessing over my diet and working out more.

This negative self-talk seems crazy to me in light of my positive thinking patterns . . . I am athletic and strong, so why do I obsess over my weight? It should be a look and feel thing. I love that I carry my weight in my butt and thighs, and I love my curves. I like my height for business, and I generally feel empowered. My natural hair is luscious and long, and I love my eyes, eyebrows, and facial structure. I truly have so much to be grateful for, and I work so hard to stay healthy, yet even in the midst of that "success" I'm constantly fixating on the negative self-talk and the ways I need to improve. I need to show myself some more love, and really commit to enjoying my cheat day and not feeling guilty about it. I want to fall in love with my own figure because it truly reflects the person inside.

Then there was an older woman who took the challenge on the eve of her seventieth birthday. She was a serial entrepreneur, and of all the participants, she was one of the few who had no problem effortlessly stating what she loved about her body. She shared:

What I'm grateful to my body for is its abilities to dance, sing, create art, and apprehend the "stuff of life" in awe. My hands create and build so many things and help me type communications to others. My feet are powerful and strong—they take me on a jour-ney of miles daily. They hold up my body so I can exude my power in a balanced and poised way. I love my mouth because it can smile and light up my day and create moments of joy for others. I appreciate my voice so that I can sing and communicate with those I love. I'm grateful for this program so that I can become even more aware of my own Bad Bitch power!

Isn't it inspiring? To see another woman freely express her love and gratitude for her own body? There is nothing selfish about loving yourself. In fact, it is the most selfless thing you can do. When you love your own body, you give other women the ability to do the same.

BAD BITCH LOVE LETTER

In the final part of the Bad Bitch Body Challenge, solidify your commitment to yourself by writing a self-love letter. If you're like me, you've tried basic affirmations and they're a hit or miss. Sure, I could stand in front of the mirror all day and say things like: "I am brave, I am strong, I am beautiful," but when I didn't actually believe it, platitudes like that just felt hollow.

In order to express genuine self-love, you have to be specific and honest. Start your Bad Bitch Love Letter by telling yourself why you're proud of the woman you've become. Think of all the experiences you've gone through, how much you've endured, and how much you've learned. Next, tell yourself why you love yourself—not because of the things you've accomplished, but because of the woman you've become. Finally, apologize to yourself for all the shit you've put yourself through, all those nasty things you've said to yourself in the past, and commit to unapologetically loving yourself going forward.

Imagine you've just put your best friend through hell only to wake up one day and realize that they're gone, and now you see all the ways you should have treated them better. Tell them you love and appreciate them as if it's your last chance to get them back.

Here's a letter one of my clients, Clara, wrote to herself:

Dear Clara,

I am so proud of you for taking a risk, starting a new venture, and stepping up as the CEO. I am so proud of you for getting up every morning and going to these meetings even when you have been rejected in the past and keeping at it. I'm proud of you for your perseverance. I'm proud of you for learning as much as you have. You've learned so much in the past year. It's amazing how much you're able to absorb and integrate.

I love you for how open-minded you are and your willingness to challenge yourself. I love that you keep a sense of humor about life, you don't take things too seriously. You bring joy and hope into the room through your words and your actions. You get so involved in the community. You don't just sit around waiting for things to happen, you always take charge and make those things happen, which is really impressive. I don't know how you do all the things that you do. I'm really amazed and inspired by all that you've accomplished. Wow, look how far you've come.

And I just want to say, I'm sorry for doubting your abilities. I'm sorry for being so critical and so down on you. I'm sorry for nagging you, that you should do this or that, or be this or that. I'm sorry for beating you up mentally about who you are and what I think you should do. I love you and I believe in you and I want the best for you. I appreciate and trust you and know you're going to do it!

Love always,
Clara

Now it's your turn. Use these prompts to help inspire you as you write your Bad Bitch Love Letter.

Dear _____,

I'm so proud of you for

_____

I love you for

_____

And I just want to say, I'm so sorry for

_____

I never should have

_____

I love you so much, and from this day forward, I promise to

_____

Love always,

_____

Challenge yourself to start each day by reading this letter out loud as you stand in front of the mirror. By doing this you are vocalizing to yourself you are worthy and deserving of love from the most important person in your life: you. Commit to this, and I guarantee this simple ritual will transform the way you show up for yourself and for others.

BAD BITCH ENERGY

Armed with your Bad Bitch Love Letter, it's time to step into your Bad Bitch Energy. In any room you walk into, your energy introduces you before you even say a word. It's essential that you learn to master your energy so you can show up and unabashedly command the respect you deserve. We don't want people to ask with indifference, "Who was that girl?" We want them to ask with intrigue, "Who is *that* Bad Bitch?"

What exactly is Bad Bitch Energy? In simple terms, it means walking with purpose, holding yourself with poise, and being fully present and open to new and exciting opportunities. Bad Bitch Energy is not overbearing in the way we've traditionally seen men take up space. When I imagine an arrogant man taking up space, I see swaggering, entitled confidence that's all ego and little substance. I think of the male entrepreneur who told me that if I wanted to get investment in my company, I needed to go into the room obnoxiously proclaiming that I'm "the greatest of all time" and that all these losers had better "man up or get out." I understand that what he meant was having unapologetic confidence and knowing my worth, but I also don't think of life as a dick-measuring contest. Plus, this way of loudly exaggerating is neither attractive nor aligned with my most authentic self, so I don't do it.

A Bad Bitch takes up space because her energy makes it clear that she *commands* the space. Contrary to the aforementioned arrogance, Bad Bitch Energy is a purposeful, poised, and present energy that is a result of knowing on the deepest level who you are, what you want, and what you bring to the table. Bad Bitch Energy consists of three distinct qualities that you must harness in order to fully experience its potency: purpose, poise, and presence.

Purpose

Maria, an executive director at a global nonprofit, came to work with me initially because she needed to work on her investor pitch. Her directive was to raise $3 million to expand their global operations, and it was her first time raising such a significant amount of money. When I asked her to stand up and do her mock-investor pitch, she started by awkwardly fidgeting with the sleeves of her baggy sweater. It was just the two of us in the room, but her anxious energy and body language already made it clear she was extremely uncomfortable.

"Hi, I'm Maria, I'm the executive director, and . . . uh . . . I'm sorry," she said. "I'm not really good at this . . . I'm not a good public speaker."

"Don't apologize," I told her. "Don't diminish yourself before you've even started."

"Oh, sorry . . . oops." She put her hand over her mouth. Apologizing for apologizing, another insecure good girl habit. She was quickly spiraling into self-sabotage, and she had barely entered the room. She was so lost in her own internal dialogue of shame and inadequacy that she had completely lost touch with her greater purpose, which was the reason she was raising money in the first place.

"Why does raising this money matter to you? What impact will it make?" I asked her. She shared the mission of her nonprofit: to prevent violence against girls and women in developing countries. The impact of the $3 million would be enormous. It would allow her to deploy a team to help install lights in numerous villages where violence against women was rampant.

Then I asked her, "How does it make you feel, knowing that these women are not getting the financial resources to be able to help themselves out of these violent situations?"

That was when she got really riled up. We tapped into her anger and passion to help her remember why she was pitching in the first place. Once she was grounded in her purpose, she was no longer worried about exactly what she was going to say, and as a result, she showed up with a different energy, believing that she had a duty to get the money—not for herself, but on behalf of other women who needed it.

The first step of cultivating Bad Bitch Energy is to get back to your own purpose. If you find yourself getting stressed or overwhelmed with all the things you have to do, zoom out and ask yourself: "Why am I doing what I'm doing? What is my greater purpose?" It doesn't matter if your purpose is to help one person or a million, think about why what you're doing matters to you. What impact will it have on others? How will you feel when you know you've put forth your best effort and created a positive impact? Whenever I feel overwhelmed, I reground myself by thinking about all the women who I have and will support to feel confident and powerful. I think back to how Good Girl Brainwashing disempowered women for centuries and the impact I can make on future generations of women. When I am grounded in my purpose, it gives me the strength to walk into rooms with Bad Bitch Energy even on days when I'm not feeling 100 percent. When you focus on your purpose, it becomes imperative that people see what you have to offer, to support you and to invest in you because a Bad Bitch on a mission requires undivided attention.

Poise

Once Maria got back to her purpose, it was time to work on her body language. Poise, the grace and power a Bad Bitch carries herself with, is the second ingredient in Bad Bitch Energy. Physically, poise can be generated through good posture, strong eye contact, and long, confident strides. In Maria's initial sessions, she came in with the exact opposite: hunched shoulders; lowered, evasive eyes; and a cautious, quiet shuffle that conveyed a desire to hide rather than take up space. As women, we already physically take up less space, being on average more petite than the average man, so shrinking ourselves when we feel insecure doesn't do us any favors. Moreover, most of us are so used to sitting bent over our computers that we literally forget how powerful we can be when we sit or stand up straight and fully occupy our space. Making ourselves smaller feels safe, even comfortable. But doing so is not what's going to get you the promotion, the investment, or the respect.

If you find yourself shrinking, it's time to walk the walk and learn the Bad Bitch Strut. Ever seen a powerful woman on a mission? She walks with purpose: shoulders back, chin up, chest out, neck long, eyes focused on the horizon in front of her. Her stride is firm and steady, a rhythmic *step, step, step* that signals authority. Her energy says, *I've got places to go, so either join me, support me, or get the fuck out of my way.*

Need a couple examples? Check out Miranda Priestly's entrance in *The Devil Wears Prada*, sunglasses on, purposeful steps, and a *no time for small talk, let's get down to business* attitude; or in *Miss Congeniality*, when Detective Gracie Hart strides out of the hangar after her makeover, hips swaying confidently despite being totally out of her element. These are women who have mastered the Bad Bitch Strut.

When I was in ballet training, my coaches would walk around continually critiquing each girl for her posture. They'd smack us across the backs of our shoulders, causing us to immediately straighten up, and anytime we relaxed, they'd smack us again, until our shoulder muscles ached from holding our posture so straight. Learning the Bad Bitch Strut doesn't require smacking, but like any other physical training, it does require body awareness and repetition.

When Maria walked into her next session, she was in for a surprise. "No pitch practice today," I told her. "Today, we're strutting." I instructed her to stand up and walk across the room. She started hesitantly, stopping halfway to look at me and ask:

"Am I doing this right?"

"Keep going," I said as I observed her small steps, raised shoulders, and timid eyes that darted back and forth. When she got to the end of the room, I instructed her to turn around and walk again.

"Chin up."

"Long neck."

"Chest out."

"Wide steps."

"Eyes straight ahead."

"Do not under any circumstances look at your feet!" I called out. She walked back and forth, back and forth, as if she were a baby deer learning how to walk for the first time. Then I pressed play on my Bad Bitch Energy Playlist. Triumphant, rhythmic beats started blaring from my phone speaker. "Strut to the beat," I directed. "Have fun! You're walking the runway. You are a sexy Bad Bitch—show me what you got!"

Maria giggled but did as instructed. She started walking with a bit more attitude, a bit more sway in her hips, her hands swinging wider back and forth. Finally, I saw the first glimmer of confidence. When she finally sat down after walking back and forth across the room dozens of times, she was breathless.

"How do you feel?" I asked her.

"I feel light. I feel energized . . . I feel free." She smiled as if she had just discovered a secret skill. The thing is, she'd had that swagger in her all along; all she had to do was learn how to bring it out and show it off.

The power of the Bad Bitch Strut is that it gets you back into your body, physically working your legs, opening up your chest, and making you aware of how you carry yourself. If you aren't used to walking confidently, it can feel weird initially, but the more you practice, the more it begins to feel normal to walk into a room and unapologetically take up the space you deserve.

Presence

Sometimes people make the mistake of thinking that bitches are snooty and cold. This is the exact opposite of what it means to be a Bad Bitch. Bad Bitches are open, inviting, and fully present to others, which brings me to the third distinct trait of Bad Bitch Energy: *presence*. Presence is cultivated by being curious, listening actively, and creating a safe, nonjudgmental space for other people to feel seen and heard. When Maria and I first started role-playing her investor pitches, she was guarded and closed off. This happened because she was drowning in her own insecurities, constantly concerned with how others might judge her. When this happened, her focus went inward and contracted her presence, signaling that she was closed to opportunities. She physically could not be present with others when she was so busy judging herself.

In order to be truly present, you must be firmly grounded in your internal worth and power. Stop overanalyzing yourself and start focusing your energy on the opportunities and people in front of you. When you are meeting with someone, silence your phone, turn on Do Not Disturb mode, and put it away. Give your full attention to the person in front of you and get curious about them as an individual. No matter someone's level of experience, wealth, or power, they are just as human as you are. Ask questions about their background, their passions, and their purpose, like: "How did you get into this field?" "What are the most important lessons you've learned in your career?" "What drives you?" Additionally, ask them how to best support them in their efforts. By actively taking an interest in their life and their goals, you are inviting them to share their full self with you, something so few people do, and in return, they will want to support you. This is how a Bad Bitch always seems to mysteriously manifest an abundance of opportunities. When you are fully present with others, you radiate Bad Bitch Energy, and they can't help but be drawn to you.

Maria and I came up with a list of questions to ask potential investors so she could be fully present and evaluate if those investors were a good fit for her nonprofit. After six months working together, practicing her pitch and continuously cultivating her Bad Bitch Energy, Maria strutted into our final session with a big grin on her face and a hefty $3 million in the bank. Reflecting on her transformation, I can't help but smile. These are the moments I live for: seeing another Bad Bitch unlocked and unleashed into the world, fulfilling her dreams with a fat check in her bank account—what could be better than that?

No matter what stage of your career you are in, the most powerful thing you can do right now is learn how to love yourself unconditionally. Repeating the daily cycle of self-loathing and self-doubt is not helping you, it is sabotaging you, and it's time to break free of it. The lessons and exercises you've learned in this chapter will help you build a strong foundation for lifelong confidence. Continue reading your Bad Bitch Love Letter and cultivating Bad Bitch Energy even in the lowest moments. You'll still occasionally have days when you don't love, or even like, yourself. Don't worry, that's normal. Even the best relationships have their ups and downs, but that doesn't mean they're not worth committing to. When you feel small, when you feel inadequate, when you catch yourself starting to go down a negative shame spiral, you know what to do: stand up, start strutting, and take up space like the Bad Bitch you are.

A BAD BITCH ASSERTS HER VOICE

UNWORTHY OF BEING HEARD

"Lisa, you're up." The event moderator, a man named Andy wearing a basic blue startup hoodie, looked at me expectantly. "Are you ready?"

I nodded, forcing myself to smile, but deep down my answer was a resounding *no*. I had spent the last month preparing for this event and was about to get onstage to do my first public startup pitch in front of a roomful of primarily white male investors, and not only did I feel woefully underprepared, I was painfully nervous.

I'm too shy.

I sound stupid.

I'm a bad public speaker.

For as long as I can remember, these were the negative beliefs I held about my voice. Even though I never expressed them out loud, they negatively impacted me throughout my early career. Starting work at a Wall Street firm right out of college, I was one of a handful of women of color. In comparison to my male colleagues, who seemed to be able to effortlessly crack jokes, tell stories, and connect with one another, I felt like a quiet outsider. I didn't raise my hand in meetings, automatically anticipating that I'd say something stupid and embarrass myself. I didn't proactively attend networking events, assuming no one would want to speak to me. I considered myself an introvert and had no idea how the extroverts around me always seemed to have something witty to say.

"How can you be shy?" people asked me. "Didn't you perform in front of tons of people as a gymnast?" Yes, *but*. I could perform physically in front of thousands of people, no problem, but I could barely speak in front of three. As a gymnast, I learned how to communicate with my body, but I never learned how to communicate with my voice.

I vividly remember the first time I started believing my voice was unworthy of being heard. I was in preschool (yes, that early), and I had been invited to a boy's birthday party. I begged my immigrant parents to spend what little money we had on an unforgettable gift for the birthday boy so he and the other kids would like me—a big deal since I was one of the only Asian girls in an all-white Midwestern suburb and did not naturally fit in. On the day of the party, we sat around a mini table piled high with gifts. He finally got to my present, a big toy truck guaranteed to create a buzz. He eagerly unwrapped the big box and jumped up in excitement.

"Whoa! It's a pickup truck! Thank you, Lisa!" he exclaimed.

I beamed and replied, "*You* welcome!"

He paused. "What did you say?"

"*You* welcome!" I repeated excitedly, until I heard one of the girls next to me snicker.

"Lisa can't speak English," she taunted. "It's *you're* welcome, not *you* welcome, stupid."

My face started burning with embarrassment. What did she mean? My parents always said, *You welcome* . . . Ah . . . in their Chinese accents. The whole table started chanting, "Lisa can't speak English! Lisa can't speak English! Lisa can't speak English!"

Their cackling, mocking voices echoed on and on. At that moment, I hated my voice, I hated my heritage, and I hated myself. From that point on, I carried with me the false belief that I was bad at speaking English, and my voice became a source of intense shame.

Even though I don't even remember the names of any of those kids, the embarrassment and hurt they inflicted didn't leave me. For years after, every time I opened my mouth to speak, especially in front of groups of people, something within me tightened in fear as my body prepared for the inevitable onslaught of criticism.

"Lisa, you're up."

The moderator's voice brought me back to reality. I stepped onto the stage, looking out at the sea of faces, and opened my mouth to speak: "Good afternoon, everyone, I—" My voice cracked awkwardly and I froze, feeling the fear gripping my body. As the heat rose up my face, I forced myself to redirect my thoughts: I reminded myself of the impact I had made with my voice when motivating my friends; I reminded myself of the positive feedback I had gotten in my practice pitch sessions; I reminded myself that I was a good writer, and words written could become words spoken. Taking a deep breath, I steadied my voice and continued my pitch with as much authority and confidence as I could muster. The pitch passed by in a blur, and to my surprise, the audience clapped as I walked offstage. *Maybe I wasn't so bad after all*, I thought. For the first time, I couldn't help but feel proud of my voice. I realized I didn't need to have the perfect pitch, I just needed to make progress, and that's exactly what I did.

Today, countless pitches and keynote talks later, I love using and sharing my voice. I am now a paid public speaker who has spoken on over a hundred stages around the world, and I have reached thousands more people through the podcasts I produce, speaking on topics ranging from confidence to investing. Through the *Bad Bitch Empire* podcast, I use my voice as a tool to share powerful lessons and as a platform to amplify other women's voices. No one ever believes me now when I tell them I used to be a painfully shy introvert.

How did I do it? By putting myself in situations where I could challenge myself to speak up. Taking the leap to become an entrepreneur forced me to transcend my own self-imposed limitations and beliefs because I realized if I was going to succeed, I had to learn how to speak, sell, persuade, and motivate. I challenged myself to stand on public stages until my voice stopped shaking. I challenged myself to go up to strangers at networking events and confidently introduce myself regardless of their reaction. To this day, I challenge myself to speak up about topics that matter to me, even when I feel uncomfortable, because I know that just one voice, including mine, can make a difference.

THE COST OF SILENCE

It's not uncommon to feel insecure about speaking up. As women, we are continually told that our voices don't matter, and the business environment is even less conducive to supporting and amplifying female voices. In the workplace, we are so frequently "mansplained" and "manterrupted" that it doesn't even register as an issue anymore. In the average business meeting, men speak 75 percent of the time, and they interrupt women 33 percent more often than other men. I guarantee that every woman has been on the receiving end of an interminable "manologue." This phenomenon isn't limited to physical meetings, either—45 percent of women say it's also difficult to speak up in virtual meetings. Why does this happen? Why are women's voices not given equal attention and airtime? Studies show that people are generally biased toward seeing women as less authoritative. This is exacerbated by both the traditional lack of women in leadership roles and our own self-fulfilling loop: When we don't speak up, we aren't taken seriously. When we aren't taken seriously, we don't speak up.

Let's not forget there's also a double standard. When we do assert our voices, we often receive backlash for being dominant, controlling, bossy, or "bitchy" (although now you can own being called a "bitch" as a compliment!). Even women in senior positions who speak up assertively are just as likely to be painted with this judgmental brush. In contrast, a man who aggressively inserts himself into a conversation is seen as a confident expert. Out of fear of being labeled negatively, we soften our language, we overapologize, we overexplain, or worse, we simply stay silent out of the false belief that it's better to be quiet and polite than speak up and potentially jeopardize our careers.

So where do we go to find professional women who can show us how to powerfully and authentically assert our voices in the workplace? Early on in my career, I tried to find business books by ambitious women who looked like me . . . problem being, I could barely find a single one. The sad fact is there are more top business books written by men named Jo(h)n or David than all women combined. To this day, women authors comprise less than 10 percent of bestselling business books. Moreover, women's stories are too often missing from business school case studies. Despite comprising 40 percent of American MBA students, more now than ever before, women are still absent in more than 80 percent of business school cases. Even when women are present, they are portrayed as less visionary, less certain, and less prone to risk-taking than men. Mainstream media publications have further contributed to this imbalance. In 2019, *Forbes* released its list of America's Most Innovative Leaders, featuring 102 founders and CEOs. Only one was a woman.

Why does this matter? Because the lack of visibility around women's stories creates major consequences. It dictates who speaks at conferences, who gets funding for their next startup, and who gets tapped for interviews and boards. When we don't have role models who look or sound like us, we start to believe our voices don't deserve to be heard, either. When we stay silent, we are perceived as not having anything useful or important to say, even when that may be the farthest thing from the truth.

How do we remedy this? At the most fundamental level, we must first learn to believe in the inherent value of our own voices. If society isn't going to support us, we must take matters into our own hands. We must assert our voices in spaces and on issues that are important to us, even if we are met with resistance. It's time to stop giving a fuck about whether or not *they* think we're nice and start speaking up about what *we* want to change.

YOUR VOICE IS A TOOL FOR CHANGE

Early on in my journey of discovering my voice, I was listening to a female entrepreneur on a panel of executives. I was struck by the way she spoke—calm and collected, her voice firm and steady. Every point she made was insightful and clearly articulated. Even when one of the audience members tried to challenge her with a difficult question, she did not waver at all, just looked him straight in the eye and shared her opinion matter-of-factly.

After the talk, I went up to her to compliment her on the discussion. I told her I loved her insights and how she connected the dots on difficult issues, then I asked her if she was currently reading any books that she could recommend. Her answer surprised me. She replied, "I'm not reading any books right now. I've spent most of my life reading other people's voices; now I want to focus on my own voice—find my own style and hear my own thoughts."

This answer blew me away precisely because I had never heard anyone intentionally focus on their voice the way she explained it, and yet it made so much sense. We spend so much time listening to everyone else's voices—reading, responding, reacting—that it rarely occurs to us to listen to ourselves.

That conversation completely changed how I saw my relationship to my voice. I knew that I also had a lot to share, and if I wanted to do so authentically, I was going to have to commit to loving, refining, and owning my voice.

I began by journaling daily, writing down unfiltered thoughts, observations, and insights as they popped up, trying my best not to judge them or myself so I could get comfortable with the voice in my head and putting those thoughts on the page. Next, I committed to recording myself speaking every morning. My goal was to acclimate myself to speaking extemporaneously, not just from a rehearsed script. I simply started recording five-minute-long voice memos once a day, every day. I walked around my room and spoke into my phone's voice recorder about any topic that came up in my head: issues I cared about, challenges I encountered, people I admired. If nothing came to mind, I would just describe an object in front of me. I was training my voice like a muscle. I stopped seeing it as something to be insecure about and instead viewed it as a tool I was sharpening to help me achieve my goals.

The more I spoke, the more natural it felt. After a week of doing this, I went back and listened to the recordings to see what patterns emerged in my inflection, my tone, and my overall speaking style. As I listened, I noticed ways to sound more confident by simply slowing down and removing common filler words such as "just," "like," "you know," and "maybe." I also discovered repetition in the topics

I talked about: entrepreneurship, personal growth, and women's empowerment frequently popped up. That's when inspiration struck: If I really wanted to challenge myself, what better way than to speak openly and publicly about the topics I cared about? Public speaking had been one of my biggest fears, but now it was time to face it: I decided to launch my podcast.

I'd already faced my fears of recording my voice, but I quickly realized this was an entirely different exercise: recording my thoughts for my own ears was one thing, but recording them and putting them out there for anybody to listen was much harder. Hitting "publish" on the first episode was terrifying, but no matter how scary it was, I kept publishing episodes and interviewing other women about their vulnerabilities and their motivations. Through the process, three powerful learnings about myself and my work emerged:

1. I wasn't alone. As I started opening up to others about my journey, I realized that many people also struggled with similar challenges, and they were grateful that I was creating a platform to discuss them.
2. I was a good interviewer! Which is something I never would have known about myself if I hadn't gone outside of my comfort zone, speaking up and talking to other people.
3. The more I spoke up and out, the more invitations I received to speak at conferences. Turns out, people really resonated with the sentiments I expressed on the podcast. Before I knew it, I was speaking on panels, sharing my voice onstage, and getting paid to talk about the topics I loved.

What my journey shows is that people can't support you if they don't see or hear you. By putting my voice out there, I was able to attract the people who most resonated with my message. I opened a channel of communication to talk about issues that other people cared about and wanted to discuss. By sharing my voice consistently, people started seeing me as an expert in my field and started inviting me to speak to their audiences. I grew to love my voice because I finally saw it for what it was: a powerful tool for connection and change.

BAD BITCH VOICE CHALLENGE

Every woman can utilize her voice as a tool. In fact, it's one of the most powerful tools we have at our disposal. Ask yourself, "What issues do I care about? What subjects am I passionate about? What unique perspectives can I share with others?"

This is where the Bad Bitch Voice Challenge comes in. It's a seven-day journey to learn how to love and express your authentic voice. The women I've guided through this exercise have shared myriad reasons for wanting to take this challenge. Some wanted to become paid public speakers or launch their own podcasts; some wanted to develop soft skills like negotiation or sales-oriented speaking to advance in their careers; others simply wanted to feel more confident speaking up in meetings and at networking events. Whatever your reason, start by committing to it:

I commit to asserting my voice so I can . . .

_____

The impact of asserting my voice will be . . .

_____

Next, it's time to record yourself. Pull out your phone and get your voice recorder ready. The challenge is to record yourself speaking about a focused topic of your choice for five minutes. Don't stop speaking until the five minutes are up, but feel free to pause throughout as you gather your thoughts. Use one of these prompts to get you started:

- I believe it's important to . . .
- The issue that I care most about is . . .
- The person I most admire is . . .
- If I could teach a class, it would be on . . .
- If I could wave a magic wand and change anything, it would be . . .

There is no right or wrong answer to any of these prompts. The goal is to get you comfortable with hearing your own voice out loud for an extended period of time. Go ahead and challenge yourself to record it right now. Remember it's just five minutes! I'll wait . . .

Done? Not so bad, right? Now go back and listen to the full five-minute recording. Objectively observe your own voice (observe, don't judge) and write down what you love about your voice and what you could improve upon in the spaces below.

I love how/that my voice . . . (e.g., I love how my voice becomes passionate when I speak about X, I love that my voice is smooth and melodic, I love that my voice is so expressive)

1. _____

2. _____

3. _____

I could improve my voice by . . . (e.g., saying "like" less often, inflecting my voice downward at the end of sentences, speaking slower and taking more pauses to breathe)

1. _____

2. _____

3. _____

Continue to record yourself every day for one full week. Each day, jot down different things you love about your voice, trying not to repeat something you wrote the previous day. As you take note of how you can improve your voice, see if you can consciously change that the next day.

Why is it important that you take this challenge? Think about the number of times you've kicked yourself for staying silent when you wanted to speak up, the number of times someone has spoken over you or taken your idea. Learning how to use your voice not only builds your own confidence, it becomes a tool you can whip out whenever you need it. Imagine the impact of sharing your ideas and finally being heard by the people who want to support you and your dreams. You owe it to yourself to speak up.

STAND UP FOR YOUR VOICE

It's one thing to build up your voice privately; it's another thing entirely to assert your voice publicly, especially in male-dominated spaces. As women, we must deal with three additional social opponents that can and often do sabotage us:

The Manterrupter: the man who unnecessarily interrupts a woman.

The Mansplainer: the man who condescendingly explains something to a woman that she already understands.

The Bropropriator: the man who takes credit for a woman's idea.

One of my clients, Elana, was dealing with all three at work. She was an analyst at a consulting firm and was having an exceedingly difficult time speaking up and being heard. She was one of two women in the group, and, despite being a top performer in her analyst class, she still found herself getting repeatedly interrupted and mansplained to in meetings. Moreover, when she shared her ideas, one of the men would quickly dismiss her, only to repeat the idea moments later and take credit for it when others approved of it.

The last straw came when he bropropriated one of her research insights and passed it off as his own, gaining undeserved praise from their boss. By the time Elana came to me, she felt defeated, silenced, and invisible. Promotion season was coming up, and she could not afford to have one more man take credit for her work. She had to figure out how to assert her voice, and she had to do it soon.

Elana started doing the Bad Bitch Voice Challenge to build up her confidence as well as one-on-one coaching sessions with me to come up with specific strategies to speak up in her aggressive work environment. We role-played the three opponents and practiced offensive and defensive strategies for standing up and responding to each one using tactics such as:

- When the manterrupter cuts you off, cut right back in without hesitation and say, "I'm not done speaking," and carry on until you have driven your point home. Conviction is key. Don't waver when you say this. If it's in person, look him in the eye when you say it, then turn back to the group to complete your thoughts.

- When the mansplainer tries to explain what you already know (most likely less eloquently than you did the first time), you want to contradict swiftly. You can respond, "Thanks for that explanation; however, that's not what I meant. The *actual* point is . . ." By pushing back, you are showing that you are confident in your knowledge and your voice deserves to be heard. No man can explain what you know better than you can, so speak up and clearly explain why your knowledge is important.

- What about the bropropriator, who steals your ideas as his own? If you know this person has a tendency to bropropriate, the ideal situation is to team up with a buddy who will speak up for you and reinforce your ideas. Someone who can say, "Elana just said that a few moments ago . . . Hey, Elana, I know you've been working on this for quite some time. I'd love to hear more about the idea from you." Make a plan with your buddy beforehand so that you both have each other's backs if the issue arises. If you don't have a buddy you can count on, you'll have to assert your own voice. Come prepared with clear evidence of the research and work you've done so you can back up your ideas. This way, even if someone tries to take your ideas as their own, you can immediately recover your position as the authority in the conversation by showcasing your expertise. Remember, it's never cool for anyone to ride your coattails and steal your hard work.

By practicing these strategies, Elana was able to build up her confidence and credibility in the workplace. She walked into meetings with talking points already in hand and made sure she was prepared with data and questions that demonstrated her expertise. She buddied up with the other woman in her group, and they both committed to supporting each other in meetings. Elana used to feel gnawing regret when she stayed silent; now, she felt powerful as she humbled the men in the room with her leadership and speaking skills. By continually standing her ground and speaking up for herself, Elana demonstrated she was the Baddest Bitch for the job and became one of the few analysts who was promoted that season.

CONFESS YOUR GOOD GIRL SPEAKING SINS

As you continue on your journey to becoming a Bad Bitch speaker, it's important to be aware of the seven Good Girl Speaking Sins. These are the most common issues I've seen that make women sound less confident and can directly undermine credibility. If you want to speak authentically and authoritatively, it's time to confess your sins and adopt new habits.

Without further ado, I present to you the seven Good Girl Speaking Sins and how to break free of them.

1. FILLER WORDS

Like, um, so, kind of, sort of, you know . . . We are guilty of using filler words when we are nervous and speaking too fast, and they have the effect of making us sound insecure and borderline submissive. If you find yourself guilty of this speaking sin, pause, breathe, and slow down. Be intentional about what you want to say, and rather than using fillers, challenge yourself to create a "powerful pause"—an extended, deliberate moment of silence that shows you are being thoughtful in what you are saying. This has the effect of making people lean in and anticipate what you are saying next rather than losing interest when you speak too fast.

2. APOLOGIZING

Stop apologizing for your mistakes, stop apologizing for being late, stop apologizing for having feelings, stop apologizing for being too much, stop apologizing for not doing enough, stop apologizing for being an inconvenience, stop apologizing for existing! Seriously, stop apologizing. As women, we've gotten used to apologizing for every insignificant thing, often for no reason. If you are doing your best, there's nothing to be sorry for. Instead of being sorry, be appreciative. Change every "I'm sorry" to "I appreciate . . ." For example, "I appreciate your understanding," "I appreciate your patience," "I appreciate your cooperation," "I appreciate it." Save your "Sorries" for things that actually require an apology. Period.

3. ASKING FOR PERMISSION

Do you find yourself guilty of questions like, "Would it be okay if . . . ? or "Is it possible if . . . ?" or "Do you mind if I . . . ?" These phrases weaken your message and status, and you can't afford that if you want to be respected like a Bad Bitch. Break free of this sin by becoming aware of instances in your daily life where you are unnecessarily asking for permission, then practice turning your permission-asking question into a statement. For example, when you are ordering your daily coffee, instead of, "Can I have a small coffee with oat milk?" say "I'd like a small coffee with oat milk, please." Or if you're trying to sit down and a man is taking up unnecessary space by manspreading, instead of, "Excuse me, do you mind if I sit here?" say, "Hi, I'd like to sit here please. Thank you." In the office, if it's someone's job to complete a task, don't say, "Would it be okay if you take over this task?" Simply say, "I'd appreciate you taking over this task because I'm tied up on a critical project. The deadline is Friday."

4. UNCERTAINTY

Ever hear someone make a solid point only to undermine themselves with the phrase, ". . . Does that make sense?" or ". . . You know what I mean?" We add these phrases to the end of our sentences when we are trying to explain something and feel we didn't do so clearly enough. Ironically, even if we did explain it well, adding an uncertain phrase at the end immediately undermines our credibility because it shows a lack of confidence in ourselves, our expertise, and our ability to communicate. The remedy for getting rid of this speaking sin is simply to remove these phrases from your vocabulary altogether. If someone needs clarification, they can ask for it.

5. DIMINISHERS

Words like "just," "a little," or "a bit"—for example, "I *just* have a quick question," or "I *just* need *a little bit* of time"—indicate to people that you think you are unworthy of taking up time and space. We usually use these phrases when we think we are inconveniencing someone. If you genuinely need someone's time and attention to do your job well, then ask, and don't be afraid to be bold and specific. Instead of needing "just a little bit of time," say, "Hey boss, I need five minutes to discuss next steps on this deal." If something is urgent and important, don't say, "It's no big deal." Instead, communicate directly and state why it's important for someone to pay attention. For example, "It's important that we get the client the deck today so we can close the deal by the end of the week," then come prepared with your talking points so you can get what you need and get back to work.

6. QUALIFIERS

Qualifiers are speaking sins we commit when we've barely even started speaking. We use phrases like "I'm not sure if it's okay, but . . ." or "I feel like we could maybe . . ." at the beginning of our sentences when we are about to propose a decision or action. Doing this downplays our suggestions so we seem less aggressive, but it has the consequence of making us appear timid and indecisive, implying our idea needs the other person's approval. Again, stop asking for someone else's permission to share your voice. Instead of hedging yourself and fearing other people's reactions, use authoritative and cooperative language to express ideas. Say "Let's try it this way . . ." or "Let's consider this option" or use data as a launchpad: "According to the data/research the best way forward is to . . ." Then if there needs to be a discussion or debate, you are coming in on equal terms.

7. THE META-QUESTION

"Excuse me, is it okay if I ask a question?" is a meta-question precisely because you are asking if you can ask a question. This is another form of permission asking, but the meta-question deserves its own category of sin because I've seen it happen way too many times. If you're in a meeting and something is unclear, don't say "Do you mind if I ask a question?" or "Sorry to bother, is it possible to just ask a quick question?" (the apologetic diminishing meta-question). If you have a question, ask it. Don't go back and commit any of the previous sins—qualifying, diminishing, apologizing. To get more information, use phrases like "Please clarify what you mean by . . ." or direct questions like "How did you come up with this figure?" or "Where do I find the source for this?" Asking sharp, incisive questions shows you know what you want and you're not afraid to ask for it.

Furthermore, Good Girl Speaking Sins also pop up in digital communication. When it comes to communicating online, it's equally important to keep things clear and concise. Remember, people have short attention spans, and with the rise of social media, they're only getting shorter. The higher up the ladder you climb, the busier people are, and the more they appreciate efficient communication. If you tend to be wordy and find yourself writing paragraphs over email or DMs, take a moment and ask yourself:

- What is the main point of my message?
- What is the one action I want the recipient to take after reading my message?

Digital communication is a means to an end, to help you do your job better, not to add unnecessary stress and confusion. My rule of thumb is no more than five sentences in emails for quick questions, and for in-depth emails that require more information, stick to five sentences and a few bullet points. For DMs or texts, keep it to three sentences or less. If you ever catch yourself starting to write paragraphs—especially about critical conversations or big decisions—quickly move it to a phone call or in-person conversation where you can showcase your new Bad Bitch speaking skills.

Which of these Good Girl Speaking Sins do you most commonly commit? Don't worry if you see a little bit of yourself in all of them. Getting conscious about how you communicate allows you to start breaking free and begin blossoming into a Bad Bitch speaker.

Bad Bitches communicate with clarity and precision: Short, sweet, to the point. There's no time to dance around the point, no need to justify ourselves, and absolutely no reason to apologize for existing. Say what you need to say, ask what you need to ask, and send the message.

If you have any lingering fear that people might not like you if you're too direct, let's release this fear once and for all. When you are direct and to the point, it doesn't make you mean or rude. On the contrary, it makes people respect you more because it signals that you value their time as much as your own. You're not making them dig through mountains of unnecessary words to try and distill what you want, and that will immediately set you apart from others.

Every time you speak up, you break the curse of Good Girl Brainwashing. Every time you assert your voice, you become a much-needed role model for Bad Bitches everywhere. You cannot afford to be silent any longer. We need your voice.

PART TWO

BOUNDARIES

"A woman steps into her full power not when she is finally given permission to do so, but when she realizes she never needed it in the first place."

—Lisa Carmen Wang

A BAD BITCH OWNS HER WINS

SILENT & HUMBLE

When I first started my career, not only did I avoid talking about my past accomplishments but I also actively hid them. I thought, *What does the past have anything to do with my present work?* Despite a consistent decade-long track record that clearly showcased my ability to work hard and succeed, I diminished myself regularly. When people asked me about my background, I used to reply:

"Gymnastics? Yeah . . . that's just a thing I did when I was younger."

When asked about my educational background, I would reply, "Oh, I just went to a small school in Connecticut."

When I launched my startup, I deflected and said, "I'm just working on a little project."

Then I would quickly deflect attention away from me:

"Enough about me. What about you?"

In my good girl mind, I thought actively downplaying my achievements and avoiding the spotlight showed my humility, but the reality is, there is a huge difference between humility and self-rejection. Without even realizing it, I was falling firmly into the latter.

Growing up in an Asian immigrant household, it was almost a given that I was going to strive for excellence and accomplish great things. My father, one of the smartest people I know, was able to move our family from low-income to upper-class precisely because he worked hard and learned how to quietly adapt to his surroundings. Parallel to his work ethic was the virtue of humility; especially in Asian cultures, humility is an honorable trait. And while it's frowned upon for anyone to be obnoxiously loud about their accomplishments, women have the additional pressure to assume an air of self-effacing deference to both their superiors and the men around them.

As an Asian American woman, the extreme pressure on me to succeed combined with my cultural conditioning to stay silent and humble meant that I was constantly at war with myself: always feeling like I had to work harder and achieve more, while never fully owning any of my wins. Even though my hard work got me far, the ugly underbelly of all that accomplishment was that I always felt inadequate. I was always so focused on what I had not yet accomplished, on everyone else who seemed to already have things figured out, that it never occurred to me to celebrate myself along the way.

It was only when I got further along in my career that I realized that I could no longer afford to downplay my accomplishments. I met male startup founders who walked around pitching multimillion-dollar valuations despite having zero revenue and nonexistent products. I spoke to a male associate who claimed to spearhead multibillion-dollar transactions even though he was only tangentially related to a project. Another man claimed to be an all-star marathoner and international athlete after running the Brooklyn half marathon once. They inflated their accomplishments so confidently that you almost had to believe them; what's worse, this kind of boldness seemed to be rewarded as I observed the less accomplished men around me continue to raise more and rise faster.

It was only after seeing this pattern play out repeatedly that I was forced to take a long, hard look at myself: I was a former USA national champion gymnast, a graduate of Yale University, a former analyst at a top-tier hedge fund, an impact-driven entrepreneur, and a Bad Bitch with an incomparable work ethic and a powerful voice. It was time I finally stood up and acted like it.

SELF-PROMOTION: ARROGANT OR AUTHENTIC?

When it comes to owning wins, I'm not alone in feeling uncomfortable. Studies show that 84 percent of women feel uncomfortable promoting themselves, 69 percent of women prefer to downplay their accomplishments instead of promoting them, and nearly 50 percent would prefer to run errands in the rain than talk about themselves in a room full of strangers (and yes, that last one's from a real study). However, this fear of self-promotion has no correlation to our willingness to put in extra time, effort, and work.

Good Girl Brainwashing encourages us to focus on working hard, being conscientious, and pleasing others. There is a visceral sense of pride that comes when we get a good grade, hit a tight deadline, or go the extra mile. It also feels good when other people tell us they can count on us; however, even though women are often cited for their ability to deliver high-quality work, many of us will go out of our way to avoid claiming credit (thus allowing the bropropriator to swoop in). In a survey of senior consulting, tech, and law executives, people were asked to rate the strengths and weaknesses of the women at their firm. Across the board, these executives cited women's strength as their ability to deliver high-quality work. But the number one thing holding them back? The feedback was unanimous: women were notoriously bad at bringing visibility to their work.

Why is this? Because in addition to being conditioned to work harder, Good Girl Brainwashing has convinced us it is arrogant and unbecoming to brag about our achievements. For fear of seeming entitled, many of us not only fail to own our wins but we also deliberately diminish our skills, experience, and contributions when asked to talk about ourselves.

Let's look at the flip side of this. Many of us have encountered that egotistical self-aggrandizing asshole who talks himself up, inflates his experience, and takes credit for things he has never done. He comes off as a total douchebag, and we sit there telling ourselves, *I never want to be that guy.* So instead, we put our heads down, perfect every last detail, and hope our work speaks for itself.

As a serial entrepreneur and investor, I see this phenomenon consistently play out in the startup world. At events where entrepreneurs pitch their companies to receive investment, male entrepreneurs often hype up their achievements, confidently sharing grand visions predicting their companies will be "the next billion-dollar unicorns" despite never bringing in a dollar of profit. Not only do they happily—and confidently—own their wins, they have no problem claiming future wins that have no guarantee of being realized.

In contrast, female entrepreneurs, who often have objectively more impressive track records, downplay their achievements and even sometimes have trouble embracing the fact that they are legitimate founders running a company and not just some lady working on "her little side hustle." While women tend to focus on their shortcomings and how they can compensate for them, men often choose to champion themselves and exude false power. The result? Even entrepreneurship, an area that purports to be an even playing field for anyone hoping to launch a business, does not provide an equal opportunity to win. To date, a paltry 2 percent of venture capital dollars are invested in female-founded businesses—not because we are any less intelligent or ambitious or worthy, but because of the way business has always been done: money flows toward power and potential, not politeness.

Unfortunately, it's also not as simple as acting like one of the bros, either. Even when we do try to own our wins, there are double standards for how women are perceived versus men. Studies show that women who promoted their achievements were seen as bad team players and were even considered a threat, whereas men who spoke of their accomplishments in this manner were admired for their ambition. When we internalize this dynamic and see other women getting berated for being too self-promotional, we subconsciously adopt the understanding that it is better to stay silent and hope others will recognize our work without having to draw attention to it.

This is especially true in male-dominated work environments where women often give more credit to their male teammates and take less credit for themselves. This is a psychological phenomenon called "attributional rationalization," in other words, the belief that "It had to be you, not me," a result of lacking confidence and relieving pressure by giving credit to someone else.

While it may seem easier to convince ourselves that being humble, downplaying our efforts, and sharing the credit with everyone else is the respectable thing to do, there are serious consequences to not owning our wins: when we don't, but the men around us do, they are the ones who end up getting the promotions, the credit, and the investment.

What's a Bad Bitch to do? How do we find the happy medium between being the invisible hero and being the cocky hotshot? How do we take credit for our work in a way that feels aligned and authentic? Enter: the Bad Bitch Pitch.

BAD BITCH PITCH

"Tell me about yourself and what you're building." I looked at Camila as she stood in front of me. Camila was fundraising for her first startup and had come to me for coaching in preparation for her upcoming investor pitches. She looked nervous, her hands fidgeting in front of her.

"I'm originally from Brazil, and I am building a fintech startup to make financing more accessible to Latin Americans." As she spoke, I looked at Camila's LinkedIn profile. She had graduated with honors at the top of her class. She was a former senior product manager with a track record of working her way up at a leading tech firm. Since then, she went on to become a founding team member of a startup that raised $20 million in funding. To top it all off, she spoke three languages—fluently.

"Anything else you want to add about yourself?" I prodded.

She paused, then responded, "Well, right now I'm just a solo founder, but I know it's important to have a partner, so I am actively looking for a cofounder who has complementary skills."

Not only did she completely skip over her impressive background, she fell into the good girl trap of volunteering her perceived weakness when I hadn't even asked in the first place. I had to snap her out of it.

"Camila, don't tell me why I should *not* invest in you. Tell me why I *should*. What challenges have you overcome? What accomplishments are you most proud of? What quantifiable wins have you had? What is your big vision and your competitive edge? I want you to tell me why you are a Bad Bitch and *own it*."

She blinked at me like she was shocked, and tried to push back, saying, "I don't want to come off as egotistical . . ." But I reassured her that was *the last thing* she would come off as. "Be authentic," I insisted. "Be honest and objective about the incredible things you've accomplished."

Finally, after a few moments of consideration, Camila took a deep breath, looked me in the eye, and proceeded to tell me: "I'm a Bad Bitch because I came from nothing and paid my own way through school. I taught myself how to code. I reached out cold and fought my way in as a Latina to have top tech firms take me seriously. As a founding team member of my last startup, I took the lead in our product department and headed up sales, bringing in our first five enterprise customers, which brought in over a million in revenue in eighteen months. I have a big vision to make financing more accessible to the Latin American market and, as a native Spanish speaker and fluent English speaker, my competitive edge is that I understand the cultural nuances necessary to succeed."

She stood there looking at me expectantly for feedback.

"Would you invest in yourself after hearing that pitch?" I asked her.

Camila thought about it for a second and nodded. "Yes, I would."

"Good." I smiled. "That's what matters."

Camila and I continued to refine and practice her Bad Bitch Pitch over the next few months. In the end, she successfully pitched her way into a top startup accelerator. Most important, she was finally able to own her wins and see herself as the Bad Bitch she had always been.

Your Bad Bitch Pitch

Before anyone else can bet on you, you have to be willing to bet on yourself. Before anyone else can recognize your wins, you must be able to recognize them yourself. There's a reason why people use the phrase "Bet on the jockey, not the horse," because it doesn't matter if you're pitching a company, a product, or a résumé—at the end of the day, people invest in people. So, the bottom line is, if you want someone to invest in you, you must unapologetically invest in yourself, own your wins, and show unwavering confidence in your ability to succeed. How do you do this? By polishing your Bad Bitch Pitch.

Your Bad Bitch Pitch is your one-minute introduction to concisely showcase just how impressive you really are. It ensures that no one (including yourself) doubts your greatness. Your Bad Bitch Pitch summarizes your mission, your track record, your quantifiable accomplishments, and your competitive edge.

When I first met Cheryl, a seasoned clothing designer at several top women's apparel brands, she introduced herself as "I'm Cheryl, a designer who's now working on a new project in women's fashion." When I dug into her actual experience, it immediately became clear that this sentence couldn't even begin to capture how impressive she was. Together, Cheryl and I worked on her Bad Bitch Pitch. Here's the result:

> I'm Cheryl, founder of a new eco-friendly womenswear startup. My mission is to empower women while also empowering our planet.
>
> I've spent over a decade professionally designing over one hundred styles of women's apparel.
>
> At my previous company, I designed the number one–selling sports bra and launched three categories of sleepwear.
>
> My designs have been sold in over nine hundred stores and have brought in $100 million–plus in aggregate revenue.
>
> Having spent my career at the forefront of this industry, I know that I have the skills and experience to tackle the $900 billion women's apparel market.

Is this an unapologetic sell of how badass Cheryl is? Hell yeah. Is it too much? Not at all. For some women, reading a pitch like this can make them feel uncomfortable because they can't imagine hyping themselves up like this. If this is you, it is very likely that you have the Good Girl Brainwashing habit of underselling yourself. That means it's even more important for you to nail down your Bad Bitch Pitch ASAP.

Let's break it down.

Your Bad Bitch Pitch is composed of the following five elements:

1. Your current role
2. Your mission

3. Your quantifiable accomplishments
4. Your competitive edge
5. Why you'll succeed

What turns a Bad Bitch Pitch into a home run? Data. A solid pitch should always quantify your wins and back up your accomplishments with hard numbers and facts. For example, a weak win would be, "I grew our company's social media following." A solid data-driven win would be, "I increased our company's social media following by 30 percent, which generated $100,000 in additional revenue." Numbers don't lie, and quantifying the impact of your contributions not only makes you feel more confident, but also helps the other person see how you bring value to the bottom line. It's not bragging if you're stating a fact.

CREATE YOUR BAD BITCH PITCH:

"Hi, I'm _____. I am (insert what you currently do)_____

My mission is to _____.

Quantifiable win #1: _____

Quantifiable win #2: _____

Quantifiable win #3: _____

As a (insert competitive edge/skills/unique experience) _____

_____ .

I'm excited to (insert big vision/why you'll succeed) _____

_____ .

Once you're satisfied with your pitch, *practice, practice, practice.* Practice pitching yourself daily until you've removed any lingering feelings of awkwardness around verbally owning your wins. If you can, find another Bad Bitch and practice your pitches with each other as you hype each other up.

After you've developed and internalized your Bad Bitch Pitch, then what? Where exactly do you deploy your newfound confidence? Think of all the scenarios where you have to introduce yourself and make a strong first impression:

- When you are pitching yourself at a professional event
- When you are pitching your startup to an investor
- When you are pitching a new client and they are evaluating whether you have the experience and credentials to help them
- When you are pitching yourself for a job interview or promotion

As women, we are rarely given the benefit of the doubt, and often have to work twice as hard for half as much. If you have a new opportunity at stake—a job, an investment, a client, a promotion—you cannot afford to sit around and wait for other people to recognize your contributions. Your Bad Bitch Pitch ensures that there is no doubt that you are a force to be reckoned with.

OVERCOME THE DENIAL DEMON

Getting your Bad Bitch Pitch down is a great first step, but the work doesn't end there. It's one thing to own your past wins, it's another to learn how to consistently celebrate your wins along the way. From personal experience, I can say that learning how to celebrate myself is one of the most unnatural habits I've had to cultivate. I grew up so used to grinding, achieving, and quickly moving on to the next thing that it never occurred to me to pause and give myself a pat on the back. In fact, instead of feeling proud of myself, I would often have this sinking sense of dread whenever I achieved something significant. I vividly remember this happening when I received my *Forbes* 30 Under 30 nomination. My friend called me and told me I had officially been chosen as an honoree. When she asked how I was planning on celebrating, I replied, "Oh I don't know . . . I still have a lot of work to do."

After I hung up, I sat there looking at my phone. Logically I knew I should feel proud, because it was definitely a win, and I knew I had worked extremely hard to get to this point in my career; however, any initial feelings of lighthearted excitement were immediately outweighed by suffocating anxiety to live up to an award that I didn't fully believe I deserved. I felt like I had fooled the world into believing that I was successful, and now there would be even more expectations placed on me that I wouldn't be able to fulfill. I shrank down in my seat, overwhelmed with self-doubt as a voice seemed to whisper in my ear, *You don't deserve this. People will find out who you really are. You're not successful enough. You're a fraud.*

You may know this phenomenon as "imposter syndrome," but I call this voice the Denial Demon. It's the devilish voice inside you that denies you any of the credit you deserve. It does this in order to make you feel inadequate and remain subordinate. The Denial Demon often shows up at the most inopportune moments, usually right when you are on the verge of feeling good about yourself. I listened to this voice for far too long, working harder and harder to prove myself worthy, until I finally realized it was sabotaging my own happiness and self-respect.

What ultimately helped me overcome the Denial Demon? Working on my sense of deservingness and acknowledging the role I played in my own success. I wrote down the decisions, risks, and investments I had made to get to this point: it was *me* who had taken the leap to build my own company, it was *me* who stayed up night after night making sure things were running smoothly, it was *me* who had defied odds to help women raise millions of dollars in funding. Moreover, taking those actions was a result of traits I had cultivated over time, including my perseverance, focus, discipline, and optimism. Of course, other people had contributed to my success—my parents, my teammates, and my community—and there is always some degree of luck involved, but that didn't mean that I deserved to be recognized any less for my success. In fact, by celebrating myself both internally and externally, I could create an opportunity to further my mission and my impact. As one of the few women of color honored in the *Forbes* 30 Under 30 Venture Capital category that year, simply by showing up and graciously sharing my win, I could be a role model and show that this was an industry in which women were on the rise and equally deserving of recognition.

YOUR BAD BITCH VICTORY LOG

The reason so many of us hesitate to own our wins is simply a lack of deservingness—the feeling that we never deserved to win in the first place. Many of us will automatically attribute our success to the support of the people around us, to luck, to timing, to anything except ourselves and the sheer hard work and dedication that got us to where we are today. By nature, successful outcomes cannot be attributed to just one thing or one person; rather, they are a result of many actions and choices that we take over the course of our lives. These can include doing your research, making sound decisions, taking continuous action, connecting with the right people, taking calculated risks, confronting difficult conversations, and prioritizing the right projects. While other factors certainly play a part in your success, I guarantee that *you* have played the most significant role. Now if you, like many women, have the tendency to undervalue your work and contributions, it's even more important to take the time to celebrate your wins.

This is where the Bad Bitch Victory Log comes in: a consistent running record of all the wins you are proud of achieving each week. As a Bad Bitch, you must learn to acknowledge yourself for both the big, obvious wins *and* the small wins—the micro actions, the micro choices—that contributed to your success. For many of us, doing this feels extremely unnatural. When we have big goals, we are always focused on what's next, what we haven't yet accomplished, which causes us to spiral into negative self-talk that continues to reinforce our shortcomings. Your Bad Bitch Victory Log reverses this by serving as a running tally, a reminder of all the ways in which you are already winning.

How do you start a Bad Bitch Victory Log? Simple: start. At the end of every day, take ten minutes—in your journal, in your notes app, wherever—to log at least three wins that you are proud of. These can be tangible results and goals you have achieved, or they can be as simple as, "I'm proud of myself for speaking up in the meeting," or "I'm proud of myself for staying positive today," or "I'm proud of myself for making it to the gym after work despite feeling sluggish."

What's important is that you are taking time to acknowledge yourself and your active role in your own success.

To help you get started, consider:

- Did you make any tough decisions this week?
- Did you have any difficult conversations?
- Did you contribute to a project?
- Did you speak up in a room?
- Did you make progress on a goal?
- Did you do something even though you didn't feel like it?

I tell every woman I work with that she needs to learn how to become her own best friend. Think about it: If your best friend lands a job she loves, what do you do? You tell her she is amazing and grab celebratory drinks. If she is going through a hard day and doubting herself, what do you say to her? You tell her she's the Baddest Bitch you know, and she can get through this. If she gets rejected, you focus on her strengths and remind her it's the other person's loss.

Your role as your best friend is to be your own hype-woman. Your Bad Bitch Victory Log is your opportunity to recognize and celebrate your best friend no matter how great or how shitty she feels in the moment.

At the end of each week, make it a ritual to read over your Bad Bitch Victory Log and treat yourself for a job well done. Not just a mental nod to yourself, but a real physical treat. Why? Because you deserve it. You have overcome obstacles, you have defied the odds, so your brain *and* your body deserve to reap the rewards.

My physical treat each week is a long, hot bath. Every Friday after work, I like to take my Bad Bitch Victory Log with me into the tub so I can internalize my wins while also associating them with a positive and relaxed physical state. Your treat can be whatever you feel like indulging in that evening—taking yourself out for a nice dinner, throwing a solo dance party, lying in bed and relaxing with a hot cup of tea. Whatever it is, it should be a treat you can give yourself every week without any additional stress, an opportunity to not only mentally celebrate yourself but also to physically revel in your strength, splendor, and success.

PROMOTE YOUR WINS

Still feel weird about celebrating yourself? Well, guess what: Owning your wins isn't just good for you, it's good for other women, too. While 85 percent of women say they feel uncomfortable promoting themselves, 83 percent said they are inspired when they hear about other women's accomplishments. So while you're building up your Bad Bitch Victory Log for yourself, do us all a favor and start owning your wins loudly and proudly out there in the world. Stop assuming that promoting your accomplishments is "bad" and instead start thinking about all the good you can do if you share your greatest gifts and your authentic self with others.

Think of it this way: If you truly believed in the value of what you are creating, why wouldn't you promote it? If you truly believed in your capacity to make a difference, why wouldn't you show yourself in the best light? When you don't own the work, skills, or perspectives that you have spent so much time cultivating, you are robbing the world of experiencing your unique gifts. If your work could benefit others, it is your duty to share what you've done. It's not selfish to promote yourself; if anything, it's selfish *not* to promote yourself.

Owning your wins is contagious, too. As we allow ourselves to stand fully in our individual power, we are setting an example and giving other women permission to do the same. By sharing openly and honestly the challenges you've overcome, the lessons you've learned, and the impact you've made, you become a role model for Bad Bitches everywhere who can look up to you and think, *If she can do it, maybe I can, too.* Sharing your success is far from selfish; it's a gracious invitation for us all to benefit from your work and celebrate your wins with you.

My client Jessica was a former SVP at a large corporation where she spent many years learning to temper herself and not outshine others. While she was more than happy to advocate for her company and her team, she never felt comfortable calling attention to herself and didn't want to offend her team members in case they felt like she was taking too much credit.

By the time she came to me, she had taken the leap into entrepreneurship, but these limiting beliefs remained. During one coaching session, Jessica revealed that she had recently become one of 1,000 women-owned businesses to receive a prestigious national grant, but she immediately tried to wave it off as no big deal.

"That's huge!" I exclaimed. "Have you shared it publicly?" She shook her head and replied that she didn't like promoting herself on social media because she didn't want people to think she was boasting. Jessica had succumbed to the false dichotomy that you must either be a self-promoting asshole or a self-sacrificing wallflower. Together, we worked through how she could confidently and authentically promote her win by:

1. Expressing genuine excitement and appreciation
2. Reframing her win so it was about her greater mission and impact
3. Presenting a call to action to support others in their journey

Her resulting LinkedIn announcement went like this: "I'm so excited to share that we are one of 1,000 women-owned businesses to be receiving this national grant. This funding will help us continue to support local and national partners with marketing, branding, and sales during a time when the future is uncertain. Contact us today if we can be of any help during this time!"

By sharing her success this way, she was not only bringing visibility to her own hard work, but she was also using her win as an opportunity to invite others to share in her excitement and feel motivated and supported.

As soon as she posted her win online, Jessica was inundated with a flurry of likes and comments: "Yay! So proud of you!" "Way to go! You deserve it." "Congratulations! You are a role model for women everywhere." In our next coaching session, Jessica revealed that she was stunned by the public outpouring of support from her community. For the first time, she realized that her hard work deserved recognition. Usually, she deflected or diminished the compliments, but this time she accepted them with a simple "Thank you" and let the well-deserved praise sink in. What's more, she revealed, "There were so many women who were genuinely happy for me. Seeing that my win could uplift others has given me even more confidence to continue putting myself out there. I realize now that celebrating myself isn't selfish, and I'm not alone on this journey." Reframe self-promotion not as an act of arrogance, but an act of Bad Bitch solidarity.

Remember, you are your own greatest salesperson, and only you have control over how you show up. If you don't own your wins, who will? Every day is an opportunity to present yourself in the best possible light—to showcase your accomplishments, experiences, and skills—so people can see exactly who they're dealing with. If someone doesn't recognize your value, move on to the next opportunity that will. Own your wins like you mean it, and don't let anyone convince you otherwise. You've worked hard and defied the odds to get here, so go ahead, step into the spotlight and let us all bask in your Bad Bitch glow.

A BAD BITCH CURATES HER CREW

THE TOXIC PARTNERSHIP

"There's no way you're going to be the CEO of our company. You don't have the qualifications; you have no idea how to lead. Besides, I didn't agree to work on this to be someone else's bitch and COO."

I looked dumbstruck at my business partner from across the table as their face twisted in anger. We had just finished meeting with an advisor and it was the first time any real conversation about titles had come up.

Sitting in that coffee shop, I ignored the alarm bells ringing loudly in my head while I tried my best to defuse my partner's extreme reaction. "Being a COO has nothing to do with being someone's 'bitch,'" I explained cautiously. "We're partners, and our work is equally important." But that only seemed to aggravate them more.

"You're weak, Lisa. No one will take us seriously if you're the CEO," they snarled back. I couldn't believe what I was hearing, but I brushed away the obvious red flags because of the other strengths I perceived in my business partner at the time—the ones I thought I lacked; this person was a go-getter, they were shameless in asking for favors and oblivious to rejection, and this had allowed us to move fast early on. Back then, I didn't have the confidence to walk away, and I thought I was doing the right thing by turning a blind eye to their behavior. But the damage was already done; this moment of conflict seeded an underlying power dynamic that became the foundation of our toxic partnership.

As we built our business, my partner often became jealous and hated the fact that I received more attention. When I was invited to speak at conferences or interviewed by the press, they would try to control my movements based on "fairness," saying things like, "You're not allowed to go to that conference. It's not fair. You went last time, so now it's my turn," or, "You have to tell the press that either we both speak or no one speaks. It has to be equal."

I tried to explain that there were plenty of speaking opportunities, and if that was something they wanted to do more of, we could work on it together; if I was specifically invited to speak somewhere, I assured them I would represent our company positively and to the best of my ability. But they wouldn't have it and accused me of trying to steal the spotlight and overshadow them.

There were other signs that this business partnership wasn't going to last. If I went to a networking event without them, they would blame me for leaving them out and trying to sneak behind their back. If I ever mentioned a prominent investor or entrepreneur I had met, they would act hurt. "Wait, you never told me about them before . . ." Then they would grill me: "Where did you meet them? When did you meet them? Why didn't you invite me?"

Over time I learned to walk on eggshells. I never knew when this person would lash out or accuse me of something new. I never knew if I might be doing something "wrong." At a certain point, they even started criticizing my clothes, telling me the things I wore were "inappropriate," and finding any chance to critique me.

Why didn't I cut ties sooner? Because there were still good moments working together. When we created new initiatives, launched valuable programs, or closed successful deals, we both couldn't help but feel proud of our progress. But even amid the highs, our relationship was never truly healthy. On the outside, our business appeared to be doing great, but on the inside our partnership was quickly deteriorating.

In our last year of working together, I developed an awful red rash on my cheek. It was angry, flaky, itchy, and started spreading across my face, down my neck, and eventually I was breaking out in eczema and hives all over my body. My rash got so bad that I felt embarrassed to even walk out in public. I tried every kind of cream, every kind of diet, but nothing worked. One specialist advised me to work less, saying it was probably a reaction to stress. By that point, the business partnership had gotten so bad that we were fighting nearly every day, and it was draining our bank account because we couldn't agree on any given strategy.

In one of our final conversations, sitting in a small, cramped conference room, my partner said to me point-blank: "If we were paid by the hour, I would be paid more than you. I am better than you." That was the final straw. My rash flared up, my face and body burning in anger, the whiplash of years of abuse catching up to me in that one moment. It finally became clear to me then: this person fundamentally believed they were worth more than me *as a human being*, and would do anything to keep me down, even if it meant destroying our business.

That was the wake-up call I needed. With a partner like that, who needed enemies? My body was shaking as I stood up from the table, but I knew I had to leave for the sake of my own health, sanity, and career. I walked out of that conference room and never looked back.

Months later, after cutting off all ties, I could finally hear myself think clearly. In the absence of the negativity and bullying, I was able to feel calm and proud of myself for the first time in years. My rash magically healed itself, and the digestive problems and insomnia that I had suffered throughout our partnership also seemed to disappear, practically overnight. My body had known all along that I was in a toxic relationship, and it had been sending warning signals begging me to listen until I couldn't ignore it any longer.

I learned the hard way that partnering with the wrong person can take a serious toll—financially, emotionally, physically, and spiritually—and that was something I could no longer afford. In hindsight, I realized I, too, had a role to play in allowing this dynamic to happen. I had lacked confidence in my own abilities, ignored red flags, and not been proactive in speaking up. Going forward, I became much more intentional about the team and network I built around me. I started listening to my gut, asking tough questions, setting hard boundaries, and cutting out anyone who didn't respect them. It took a toxic relationship to help me get there, but after a lifetime of trying to please others, I finally developed the strength to prioritize myself before investing in anyone else.

ROLL WITH WINNERS

Good Girl Brainwashing teaches us to put the needs of others before our own. It teaches us to suppress ourselves, rather than rocking the boat; to sacrifice ourselves, rather than listen to our instincts. The result is good girls often end up in bad scenarios with people who drag us down rather than lift us up. In many cases, our bodies become aware that we are in the wrong situation long before we consciously do. In any unhealthy dynamic, we often have that gut feeling that someone isn't good for us. Even if we override that feeling, our bodies continue to warn us through symptoms like anxiety, pain, breakouts, insomnia, digestive problems, panic attacks, and more until we are forced to face the facts. Other times, we stay in unhealthy situations not because we are unaware that they're bad for us, but because we've been trained to feel guilty for leaving them.

I stayed in my toxic business relationship as long as I did because I wanted so badly for our business to succeed, to the point that I was willing to do anything to make it work. I falsely believed that splitting up would mean I was failing, that I was letting down my team; only later did I realize that by sacrificing myself, I was also hurting others. By participating in my ex-partner's drama, I couldn't show up fully for any of our teammates or our projects. By settling for someone who was inherently distrustful, I became distrustful as well, which affected my ability to communicate authentically and openly. By constantly being around their negative energy, I too became more self-critical and judgmental of myself and others. The whole time I was in that partnership, I lived in a constant state of fear and vigilance, afraid that I would do something wrong, rather than thriving in a state of power and trust—the place I needed to be in to maximize my opportunities and grow as a leader. I made the mistake of settling for shitty behavior, and not only did it cost me my physical and mental health, I became a shadow of the woman I knew I could be.

As Bad Bitches, we cannot afford to settle for mediocre behavior and average people who will drag us down. The people you associate yourself with shape who you become. They determine the conversations that dominate your attention and the attitudes, opinions, and behaviors you adopt. If you're around people who are insecure, negative, and critical, you will become insecure, negative, and critical. On the flip side, if you're around people who are confident, positive, and empowered, you will also become confident, positive, and empowered. Studies show that the people you spend the most time with can determine as much as 95 percent of your success or failure in life. If you're a Bad Bitch with big dreams, it is critical to start paying attention to how you curate your crew both professionally and personally.

Who exactly do you want in your crew? You want winners. Winners are people who empower you, support you, and celebrate you. They make introductions, open doors, cheer for your success, and act as springboards to accelerate you in your career. When they see your vision, they ask, "How can I help?" When they see you succeed, they cheer, "Hell yes, keep rising!" When you join forces with winners, the opportunity for growth, success, and fulfilment become exponentially greater.

The people who don't fit into this category? The ones who distract you, criticize you, and undermine you. These are the haters who purposely harm you, the frenemies who secretly sabotage you, the critics who actively condemn you, or the losers who simply hang around and add no value to your life. Being exposed to the wrong people for long periods of time—especially if they're negative, envious, creating drama, or keeping you from your goals—will ultimately lead to your downfall.

Now that you know what's at stake, take a long hard look at your current surroundings, specifically think about the friends, partners, or colleagues you surround yourself with: Are the people around you lifting you up or bringing you down? Are they encouraging you to grow or holding you back and telling you to play it safe? Do they inspire you to be bigger, better, and bolder? Or do they plant seeds of doubt in your mind before you can even begin to dream of what's possible? These questions are applicable to all parts of a Bad Bitch's life, so carefully consider the positive or negative patterns of anyone you spend significant time with; sometimes the people closest to you are the most harmful. If you really listen to your gut, you'll know whether someone is adding or subtracting value from your life.

Schools teach you that there's no shortcut to success in life, but they're wrong. The one shortcut they never teach you in school is this: at some point, it's not about how much you do; moving up is about who you know and who you surround yourself with. Even if you've worked hard to get to where you are now, there's only so much you can do alone or with a mediocre crew. Getting to the next level means intentionally building a team of winners around you who see your value and want to help you grow.

YOUR CORE VALUE SYSTEM

When I coach startup CEOs, one of the first things we do is develop their core value system. These are the three nonnegotiable values they set for themselves and the team that they're building around them. CEOs with clearly defined values have a much higher chance of success because they can identify and hire the right talent, save time making decisions, and quickly cut their losses.

For example, one of my CEO clients, Rina, came to me because she was growing her team but was struggling to find the right talent. After going through several rounds of interviews with multiple candidates only to figure out weeks later they weren't the right fit, she realized she had to find a better way. "It's not that they don't have the right skills," she said, "it's just that something doesn't exactly fit . . ." Her intuition was telling her "no," but she needed a more clearly defined rubric. Together, we sat down to clarify three core values that she wanted her team to embody.

First, I asked her, "What do you think are your most admirable qualities?"

She replied, "I think my most admirable qualities are that I'm relentless. I am always challenging myself to try new things. I'm also super curious, so I'm always discovering new ways to grow."

Next, I asked her, "In your ideal business partnership, what is most important to you?"

Without hesitation, she responded that the most important thing for her is to have clear and transparent communication. "I've been in partnerships with people who hid things and became passive-aggressive. I can't handle that. My ideal partnership is one in which we can openly share how we feel even if we disagree and come to a good solution."

Finally, I asked her, "How do you want yourself and your work to be remembered?"

She replied, "I want to be remembered as someone who worked hard to create a big impact. I get the most joy out of work when I know I'm creating a real positive impact in other people's lives; that's why I'm building a company where I get to do that."

Through these questions, she was able to identify "growth," "transparency," and "impact" as her three core values. She was then able to apply these core values to developing her company culture, hiring new team members, and surrounding herself with people who also aligned with her values. To foster "growth" on her team, she evaluated potential hires on their level of curiosity and flexibility and scheduled regular brainstorming sessions to allow diverse ideas to surface. To ensure "transparency," she held weekly team meetings where team members could openly ask about the company's direction and strategy. She also owned up to her mistakes as the CEO to inspire others to do the same. Finally, "impact" became a key part of the interview process, and she would carefully evaluate candidates on why they wanted to join the company, and if they didn't bring up the mission, she immediately knew that it wouldn't be the right fit.

Having clearly defined values made it much easier to identify the types of people Rina wanted to have on her team versus the ones she didn't. By finding clarity on how those values tangibly showed up in her company culture, she was able to efficiently identify and onboard her new chief marketing officer, a position that was critical to the growth of her business.

Define Your Values

Now it's your turn. Even if you're not the CEO of a company, you are the CEO of your life. Like any great CEO knows, the team you build can make or break you. Whether you are bringing people onto your team or considering joining someone else's team, by clearly defining your values, you create boundaries around the behaviors and actions you will or will not accept.

To figure out what your values are, fill out the blanks below.

The qualities I admire most in myself are . . .

1. _____

2. _____

3. _____

In my ideal business partnership, the most important things to me are . . .

1. _____

2. _____

3. _____

I want my work and myself to be remembered as . . .

1. _____

2. _____

3. _____

Once you've written down your answers, you should have a series of potential values to choose from. Spend time thinking about which three are the most important to you, and these will become your core value system of nonnegotiables that you want to hold yourself and others to. If you're still having trouble, here are a set of values that you can use as a jumping-off point, or feel free to create your own:

Accountability

Boldness

Collaboration

Consistency

Curiosity

Diversity

Honesty

Humility

Growth

Impact

Inclusion

Innovation

Integrity

Passion

Persistence

Self-improvement

Sustainability

Teamwork

Transparency

Trust

Vulnerability

Once you've selected your top three, refer to the following questions to help you understand how each of these values manifest in your life and work:

- In what ways do you personally exhibit these values?
- How will you be able to tell if someone is aligned with these values? What behaviors do they exhibit or not exhibit?
- What are red flags? Absolute deal breakers?
- What questions can you ask to figure out if this person is aligned with your values?
- What does someone who embodies the opposite of this value do?

By clearly defining your values and having the answers to these questions in your back pocket, you'll be able to efficiently evaluate situations and people and easily set boundaries around your time and energy. People who are clear and consistent in their values are rare. If you are committed to your values and unwavering in your boundaries, it will pay off because it shows that you respect yourself, and that will ultimately attract the right people toward you. And the ones who don't respect you for it? Well, they didn't belong in your crew anyway.

FULL-BODIED "FUCK YES"

"I'm thinking of taking money from this investor," Yasmin confided in me during one of our coaching sessions, "but I felt kind of uncomfortable after our meeting." Yasmin was another one of my startup CEO clients who was raising her first round of investor money. She had already raised some initial capital from a couple of investors but needed two more significant checks to close out her round. This last investor had a brand name that was reputable in the industry and had shown a lot of interest in Yasmin's company, but she had left feeling inexplicably anxious. Rather than brush it off, I dug into why she felt that way. "I think I just didn't like the questions they were asking me. They were so focused on the revenue, costs, and financial projections, but they didn't seem to care much about the product we were building and how it could genuinely help our customers."

Yasmin was building a company to help independent artists create new sources of revenue through the blockchain. As an artist herself, she was extremely passionate about the greater mission of uplifting the artist community; the fact that the investor seemed to care much more about the business model than the mission made her feel uneasy. However, she knew this was an investor with a good reputation and was flattered that they were interested in investing in her in the first place. Besides that, she had been raising money for months and was itching to close out her first funding round. So she initially ignored her gut and continued taking meetings. After several more meetings with this investor, they were ready to invest, with one stipulation: they wanted to push down her company's valuation and take a bigger ownership stake to have more say in the company's growth strategy. This rang loud alarm bells in Yasmin's head.

When I asked her how she felt about their proposal, she replied, "I don't know. They've got a big name in the industry. Everyone else says I should take the money . . . so I'm considering it." The rational arguments were getting the best of her, especially because she knew this was a well-known investor who might be able to bring a lot of social value to her company; however, I told her she deserved to sit and listen to what her body was telling her. This wasn't a small decision— taking money from an investor is not unlike getting married. It's a long-term legal commitment with clearly defined expectations, not a blank check with no strings attached. Just like how you don't confess your love on the first date, you also don't bring on a key business partner or investor without seriously considering compatibility. There was a reason Yasmin was feeling uneasy about going into the deal, so she needed to realign with her core values.

Turns out, as an artist turned entrepreneur, two of her core values were "creativity" and "independence," and she realized taking money from this investor would be in direct conflict with these values. When she had asked the investor how involved they'd like to be, they said they needed a board seat and needed to have a lot of input into their companies, which implied a lot of control. What's more, the decreased valuation they wanted would mean less ownership for Yasmin and her current team. On paper, it was a great investor to get, but when we went back to her core values of "creativity" and "independence," she realized that if she let this investor in, she would lose much of the creative freedom she had fought so hard for. Despite all this, she was still waffling, so I finally asked her: "Is this a full-bodied 'fuck yes' for you?"

A full-bodied "fuck yes" is more than a "yes." It is when your physical and mental states align and you can say without hesitation that this person, place, or thing feels absolutely right for you. When I feel a full-bodied "fuck yes," for example, my breath slows down; I feel calm, grounded, at peace. I feel enveloped in warmth. When it's a "maybe," or a "no," the opposite happens. I feel anxious and uneasy, my breathing inadvertently becomes faster and shallower, and my senses feel like they're on high alert.

When the question was framed that way, Yasmin instantly knew her answer. "No, definitely not." She shook her head firmly and exclaimed, "My head was saying 'maybe,' but my body is saying 'hell no!'"

"Well, there you have it," I told her, "If it's not a full-bodied 'fuck yes' for a decision as important as this one, it's a no. There's plenty of money out there—you deserve to have only 'fuck yes' partners on your team. Do you believe you deserve that?"

Yasmin nodded. With that in mind, the decision was clear. Even though this investor could provide the money and reputation she needed, she knew she had to let them go. Even though others thought it was risky to turn them down, Yasmin stayed true to herself by refusing to settle for anything less than a "fuck yes." She prioritized her values and decided not to take the money. A month later? She found her full-bodied "fuck yes" investor. Not only was this new investor extremely excited about the product and aligned with Yasmin's mission, they loved the fact that she was able to infuse her creativity into the business model.

Next time you're at a crossroads of an important decision, pause and listen to your body. What information is it sharing with you? What energy is it picking up that your rational mind might not have access to? It can take time to fully process all the signs your body is giving you, so be careful not to make serious decisions when you are in an emotionally charged state, whether negative—stressed, sad, angry, desperate, tired, or afraid—or positive—euphoric, excited, in love, or starstruck. Not only can you not think clearly when heightened emotions take over, but you also cannot fully sense what your body is telling you. Give yourself the time and space to feel out all those little indicators that your body is giving you. Ask yourself, *Does this really feel good for me?* and trust that your body will guide you toward the right answer.

LEVEL UP YOUR CREW

As you evolve in your life and career, the people you surround yourself with will also inevitably evolve. The best friends you grew up with, went to school with, or started your career with will start going down their own respective paths, and the ones who you thought would be in your crew forever may gradually start to drift away. It doesn't mean anyone is right or wrong, it just means it may be time for you to explore a new crew, especially if you want to achieve your Bad Bitch Dream.

When I took the leap into entrepreneurship, I struggled with this frequently. Many of my peers didn't seem to fully understand what I was doing, why I was working so hard, and just how much effort went into launching a new company. While I still cared about them, what I really craved was a community who deeply understood, admired, and uplifted each other's dreams; a crew that could have fun together on a personal level *and* add strategic value to each other's career aspirations. Moreover, as a new entrepreneur I had a lot of questions about everything from fundraising to hiring, and I needed experienced entrepreneurs and advisors around me who could guide me in the right direction. I realized that if I wanted to level up, I couldn't just wait around for these people to appear, I had to be proactive in cultivating a new community around me, so that's exactly what I did.

I started by looking for role models, entrepreneurs who had accomplished big goals similar to the ones I was hoping to accomplish. I read articles about them, listened to their stories on podcasts, and learned about their interests on social media. I found out the events they were speaking at and made sure I was in the audience, ready to ask insightful questions and make an impression. When I reached out, I made sure to not just ask for advice but also to express my admiration for their work, and see how I could support them. By being proactive, genuine, and gracious, I gradually started to build up a powerful network of like-minded builders and hustlers who would help me succeed.

In fact, not only did I build a network, I built an entire business out of my desire to level up and be around powerful female entrepreneurs. My previous company, SheWorx, started with a small group of eight women at a coffee shop, and blossomed into a community of over twenty thousand female entrepreneurs. By creating a stage for women to share their respective entrepreneurial journeys, I was able to amplify their voices and help them fundraise; in turn, they empowered me to grow. Then, when I dove into the male-dominated world of crypto, I realized I once again needed to level up. I wanted to learn how to find legitimate projects, build a diverse portfolio of investments, and find like-minded women in the web3 space who wanted to invest and grow together. When I realized I didn't have those friends in my immediate circle, I got proactive. I began educating myself on blockchain technology, identifying role models, and then built another powerful program, the Bad Bitch Bitcoin Bootcamp, to share knowledge and cultivate my badass crew of Bad Bitch crypto investors.

No matter where you are in your career, it's important to think about who you're surrounding yourself with in the context of achieving your goals. If you want to level up and create your dream crew, you must be strategic and intentional. Start by thinking about who you want to be in your crew:

- Who are the types of people who can help you achieve your dreams?
- What kinds of skills, experiences, or perspectives do they have?
- What industries are they in?
- How do they add strategic value to your life?
- How do they make you feel when you're around them?
- What qualities and values do they embody?

It's totally fine to think about how someone can strategically add value to your life. A strategic friend doesn't make someone an inauthentic friend; in fact, the more I've grown in my career, the more I've found that every new friend I bring into my crew has something to offer. Because we respect and admire each other, we inevitably want to find ways to add value and be a part of each other's journeys. Once you've figured out the types of people you want in your crew, identity specific role models and start researching them:

- Who are individuals you admire?
- What do you admire most about them?

- What specific traits about them do you want to emulate?
- What can you learn about them from social media? Press? Podcasts? Blogs?

Once you've created your target list, it's time to take action. Figure out what conferences or events your role models are at. Get a ticket, sit in the audience, and go up and greet them. Find their online webinars and be the first to ask questions. And if you can't physically get to them, reach out cold via email or DMs. Be authentic in your message and always think about why someone would bother to respond to you. Ask yourself:

- How can I show I've done my research on them?
- What kind of value can I offer to them?
- What would make this person excited to speak to me?

One of the greatest rookie mistakes is to cold email someone you admire and ask if you can "pick their brain." Whenever someone uses this phrase, I cringe because it is so cliché and it completely disrespects the other person. If someone has worked hard to be successful, why would they allow you to just "pick their brain" like a piece of trash off the sidewalk? Whoever you're reaching out to is likely very busy, and even if you send a cold email, they will gloss over it unless you find a way to be valuable to them. Show that you've done your research on them, tell them why you admire their work, ask how you can support them, offer to do something for free, be flexible, and if you have the opportunity to meet them, be ready to ask great questions to show you are serious about leveling up. Remember, you get what you give, so if you share your passion, curiosity, and commitment to growing, people will sense that and want to help you grow.

Finally, as you level up in your career, make sure to regularly reevaluate your crew. If you find you've outgrown certain people or groups of people, it is okay to move on. It doesn't make you a bad person, it just means you are learning to prioritize yourself and being intentional about where you spend your time and energy. Especially if you find people in your past are holding you back or jealous that you're growing, know that it's not about you, it's about them. In some cases, you can slowly phase the relationship out; in others, you just have to cut them out cold turkey so you can reallocate your time accordingly.

As a Bad Bitch, it's important to hold others to the same standards you hold yourself. There's absolutely nothing wrong with having high standards, so never allow anyone else to persuade you otherwise. At the end of the day, you are who you surround yourself with, so make sure that the crew you're curating around you is unequivocally a full-bodied "fuck yes" influence in your life. You deserve nothing less than a Bad Bitch crew that wants to see you soar.

A BAD BITCH CALLS OUT BULLSHIT

"TRUST ME"

The first time I realized I had been manipulated by a trusted male mentor, I was stunned. He was decades older than me, and it had never crossed my mind that he had any ulterior motives.

He complimented me: "You're so wise for your age."

He expressed interest in my growth: "You have so much potential."

He wanted to help me succeed: "You should meet the people in my network."

He offered me valuable access and advice.

He was powerful, rich, and well respected. He made me feel seen in a way that peers my age didn't. I was voracious to absorb his experience and wisdom in hopes that I could advance faster in my career. Every time he turned his gaze upon me, I felt lucky that he chose to share his mentorship with me over anyone else.

"Trust me," he said, so I did.

I only began to realize he had intentions beyond being my mentor when I began to pay attention to the little things. I noticed how his eyes would scan me up and down when I walked into meetings, subtly taking me in from afar. It wasn't unusual for him to pay me compliments about my appearance. At one meeting, he said, "That dress hugs your body beautifully," as I took the seat across from him.

"Thank you," I replied dutifully. The compliments never felt creepy; if anything, they felt well deserved. After all, I liked my dress, too.

Then I started noticing how frequently he texted me, and the offers he made me, which always carried a sense of urgency.

"Come out with me tonight. You need to meet this investor, but first let's grab a drink."

"There's a private event tonight; you'll meet very important people. Come now."

"You should speak at this conference. Let's strategize your pitch today. Meet me here."

No matter what I was doing, I dropped it. I answered his call, "I'll be there."

Even if it was late, I ignored the tug of discomfort in my stomach. Because the people he introduced me to *were* powerful. The events he took me to *were* exclusive. The insights he provided me *were* useful. But what I didn't realize was that he was getting something valuable in return.

He was getting my time, my attention, my admiration.

He was accumulating my trust, my loyalty, my indebtedness.

He was gaining a trainee, a disciple, and a young woman he could manipulate.

This man knew I was smart, but he also knew what I was driven by, so he baited me with what he knew I needed to feed my ambition and intellect, all the while slowly securing my dependence on him.

The first time he put his hand on my thigh, he did so smoothly while looking me in the eye and offering me the promise of an investment. I froze. Alarm bells started ringing in my head. He knew what he was doing. He knew how badly I wanted the investment. "Trust me," he said, "I'll help you succeed." I nodded numbly. "Good girl," he said approvingly.

Back then, I didn't have the strength to call out the bullshit that is so obvious to me now. I believed he had more to offer me, I believed he was more important than me, so I stayed silent and accepted the harassment. I allowed him to have power over me, and throughout it all, despite my gut telling me I shouldn't, I still felt grateful—grateful that he was giving me his mentorship, grateful that I had finally earned his investment, too.

It wasn't until I started holding him accountable to his word that the cracks finally started to show.

"Can you confirm your investment?" I messaged him weeks later. "Other investors are asking."

"Yes, he replied. "You can let them know I'm in. *Trust me*."

I read the message and felt his glow of approval shining down on me. I announced proudly to my close network that after months of hard work, I was finally closing my investment round.

And then he dropped the bomb.

He wanted new terms. In exchange for his investment, he now wanted to own 51 percent of the company. That meant he would have a controlling stake in my company's future. In *my* future.

It wasn't the company he wanted to own.

He wanted to own *me*.

For weeks, I grappled with the decision to accept or reject his new terms. The fact that I even seriously considered them shows just how much influence he had over me. Eventually, I came to my senses when I realized I was being inconsistent with my core values. This was not a full-bodied "fuck yes." I could not accept his investment. Unsurprisingly, he was not happy at all, and after a slew of angry messages, I eventually cut off all communication.

Months later, I was still silently struggling. I continued to berate myself: *How could I have been so stupid? How could a woman like* me *end up in a situation like* this? My silence stemmed from the belief that I was fully at fault for my mentor's manipulation, and my shame was the reason I couldn't bring myself to speak about it as I tried to dig myself out of the hole he had put me in. When I finally shared the news that my key investor had dropped out, it was too late. The damage had already been done. While I was forced to deal with the financial repercussions, he suffered zero consequences for his actions. Consumed with feelings of guilt, embarrassment, and fear, I—like so many women before me—hid in the face of harassment. I learned the hard way that abuse of power can and does happen, and if you have weak boundaries, the wrong people *will* take advantage of you.

THE SILENT COST OF HARASSMENT

For too long, women have silently harbored horror stories about sexual harassment in the workplace. Encounters with powerful men—

our bosses, colleagues, investors, advisors, and mentors—can and often do transform into inappropriate interactions in which lines are blurred and power dynamics are abused.

In 2017, workplace harassment came bursting into the spotlight when Susan Fowler, now known as the Uber whistleblower, published a lengthy blog post titled "Reflecting on One Very, Very Strange Year at Uber," in which she detailed the various types of abuse and harassment she experienced during her time as a software engineer. These included inappropriate remarks, sexual propositions, and attempts at blackmail. Even after reporting her experiences to HR, not only was no action taken on her behalf, they purposely deflected and brushed Fowler's complaints under the table. Unfortunately for Uber, the swift response by hundreds of women to Fowler's blog post revealed that this was not an isolated company incident, but rather an unsettlingly widespread occurrence across the tech and financial industries.

Once that first domino fell, others followed suit. A year later, what started as "one very, very strange year" became a national movement as women in media also began calling out some of the most powerful men in the industry for decades of harassment. Within a year of going official, the #MeToo hashtag was used over nineteen million times on Twitter.

Since then, there has been increasingly more lip service addressing this issue publicly. Many workplaces now adhere to anti-harassment policies and training to show their commitment to creating a safe workplace for employees; however, reality reveals the disappointing truth. Sexual harassment in the workplace is still appallingly common. As many as 69 percent of women have been sexually harassed in a professional setting, with over 80 percent of them being harassed by someone at a more senior level in their organization. What's more, over 70 percent of disabled women and LGBTQIA+ workers also report experiencing sexual harassment at work.

Unfortunately, the abuse doesn't stop at physical harassment, either. Verbal harassment is rampant in American workplaces. The data ranges, but in general, 77 percent of women experience verbal harassment, and 51 percent of women are physically touched without permission in professional settings every year. Since the Covid-19 pandemic forced office-job employees into working remotely, with workplaces switching to online communication as a result, women reported increased inappropriate sexual messages—emails, texts, social media—as well as calls and online harassment directly through company communication tools like Zoom, Slack, Microsoft Teams, and more. Clearly, even physically removing ourselves from toxic work environments doesn't prevent this bullshit from happening.

Even though we aren't at fault for the abuse we experience, women have been gaslit to believe we are. When we reflect on our past run-ins with the office creep or the handsy boss, we often can't help but feel crazy, overdramatic, and downright stupid. Women who have tried to report their stories have often found themselves mocked, silenced, ignored, or worse: women are fired, blackmailed, and torn apart by the media, and have their careers derailed for speaking up. Reputations are smeared, and some women are even excommunicated from entire industries if their abusers are powerful enough.

As a result, many women choose silence. Close to 85 percent of victims never file a complaint with HR or press charges, and across the board, only 1 percent of victims ever confront their perpetrators. And even when we do? Most male perpetrators get nothing more than a slap on the wrist. So, when given the choice, few women ever discuss their experiences with coworkers or superiors and instead opt to suffer in silence, or even take it upon themselves to quit their jobs or work for a different company, forced to watch on helplessly as their abuser walks free and continues their trail of destruction.

On the one hand, companies need to be held responsible for creating safe workplaces and enforcing consequences because, guess what?

Sexual harassment is expensive for them, too—costing $2.6 billion in lost productivity and nearly $1 billion in other financial costs annually.

On the other hand, we as Bad Bitches cannot rely on legacy systems that don't have our best interests at heart. We need to protect ourselves and other women first and foremost. We need to call out bullshit when we see it, and we must be strategic when doing so. We need to understand the types of bullshit we're dealing with, assess what is or is not within our power, and rally the right support around us to give us the greatest chance of coming out on top. By speaking up, we are not only looking out for ourselves, but for all of us who deserve safe workspaces.

BLURRED LINES TO BLATANT VIOLATIONS

"Wow, I had no idea women had to deal with that . . ." my friend Adam, a fellow entrepreneur, replied in shock after I shared with him my past harrowing fundraising experiences. He continued, "When I pitch investors, all I have to think about is whether or not my company sucks. It never occurs to me to wonder if they are going to hit on me." Then to show his support, he uttered a few meager words of reassurance: "That sucks. I'm sorry." Even as a male "ally," it was clear that he could not fully empathize or comprehend the gravity of the situation.

The sad reality is, as women, there are countless factors we must consider when navigating professional situations where men are in power. Factors that most men rarely, if ever, have to contend with. The extra mental burden that comes from having to think about things like *What should I do if he hits on me?* is only the beginning.

Instances of harassment happen so often and have been so normalized that sometimes we don't even realize when our boundaries have been violated, especially when it comes to the quick and dirty violations—the "accidental" boob graze, the casual ass grab, the not-so-PG sexual joke. From blurred lines to blatant violations, harassment is anything that crosses your boundaries—physical, emotional, personal, or professional—without your consent.

To put it explicitly, here is a short list of bullshit I experienced in the first few years of my career:

- Ass slap at a professional event
- Sexual comments about my legs and breasts
- Dinner dates disguised as "mentor sessions"
- Unsolicited good-night kiss
- Inappropriate sexual jokes
- Hand slid onto my thigh under the table
- Withholding help if I didn't give myself up
- Sexual comments about my outfits in meetings
- Rubbing up against me at a networking event
- Hand on my lower back at the bar
- Sexual blackmail
- Side boob hug
- Sexual offers and gifts

That's just the short list, and I'm certainly not alone. When I shared a survey to the women in my community and asked them to share their experiences, the responses were overwhelming and endless. While each story had its own unique flavor of abuse, there was no shortage of repeated offenses.

When I was leaving a work dinner, my colleague walked me out. As I said goodbye, he leaned over to try and kiss me. I turned my head to the side and his mouth landed on my cheek. It all happened in a split second. The next day he acted like nothing happened, but it was so awkward and uncomfortable for me.

Throughout my career, every time I walked into the room, I heard guys saying things like "leg," "ass," "rack." I would just try and ignore them and go on with my presentation, but I constantly felt objecti-fied and like I wasn't being taken seriously.

In the final presentation for my company, one of our investors reached over and grabbed my breast. I was in shock. The crazy thing is there were other people in the room who saw and no one said anything.

My boss called me into his office, and I thought it was to review one of the projects I was working on. He told me he always found me attractive then straight up asked me to have sex with him. I couldn't believe what I was hearing. He's married with kids, so I thought he was a good guy. I was wrong.

Just remember the old saying: "Everything is about sex, except sex; sex is about power." While this may be a controversial and unap-pealing way to frame things, the reality is it doesn't matter if you're wearing a turtleneck or a revealing dress, an abuser will still try to find a way to violate you. To be clear, I'm not negating good men who have genuine intentions to support you, but for your own sake, it's better to be safe than sorry and question what you are presented at face value. That tug of discomfort you're feeling? It's your intuition trying to communicate to you. When in doubt, listen to it.

IDENTIFY THE BULLSHITTERS

Having now encountered my fair share of bullshit, and having heard so many stories from other women, I've distilled some of the most common types of bullshitters and the tactics they use to lure us into sticky situations (before gaslighting us into thinking otherwise). Take notes and watch out for yourself and the women around you.

The Pressurer

This is the man who uses pressure as a psychological tactic to manipulate a woman's ability to think rationally and settle for a situation that is not in her best interest. There are three key types of pressure that he applies: 1) Time pressure; 2) Social pressure; 3) Authoritative pressure.

I was once at an evening networking event and a man started chatting with me. He took an interest in my business, asked thoughtful questions, and throughout the interaction gave me good reason to believe we were having a productive professional conversation. Midway through, he casually mentioned he was heading to the next event.

"Do you want to come with me?" he asked.

I was hesitant. I had just met this man, and I didn't have enough information about the next spot to be sure, so I responded, "I'm not sure."

Unsatisfied with my answer, he attempted to apply social pressure on me. "Oh, come on, it'll be fun," he said. It's where *everyone* is going after this."

"Everyone?" I asked.

"It's a VIP event with the *right* people," he said. Then, applying authoritative pressure, he proclaimed, "This is the kind of event you *need* to go to if you want to move up." His condescending tone rubbed me the wrong way, so I shifted my body away. He sensed it, so he used his last tactic: time pressure. He looked down at his phone and abruptly moved toward the door to signal he was going to walk. "The Uber is going to be here in one minute. Are you coming or not?" He was using urgency to shift the power dynamic and force me to make a rushed, uninformed decision.

For a second I wondered, *Should I just go? Maybe it's actually a good opportunity.*

He made one last attempt and doubled down on the time pressure. "Hurry up, the car's here. Last chance." I didn't move. He shrugged and rolled his eyes. "Your loss," he said and walked away. That was the moment I knew I had made the right decision.

Applying urgency is especially effective because it negates the amount of time to weigh the pros and cons and forces you to make a snap decision before you can really listen to how you feel. It becomes even more influential when it's done by a superior or when you are under the influence of alcohol. Get familiar with these three types of pressure so you don't give in to them when they are used on you. If someone is applying unnecessary pressure, you can use a deferral tactic—step aside for a moment to use the restroom or ask them to message you how it is once they get there. Once the person is out of your space and the pressure element is gone, you can evaluate the opportunity from a more grounded state.

The Neg

The Neg is an insecure man who "negs" women, in other words, puts her down in order to feel like he has an advantage over her. Negging is a form of emotional manipulation to play off your insecurities, make you feel less confident, and put the Neg in a position of power over you. A few common forms of negging:

- **BACKHANDED COMPLIMENTS:** As opposed to a true compliment, backhanded compliments manipulate you into feeling insecure by pointing out something wrong with you but disguising it as a compliment. "You did a great job, although I'm surprised you were able to handle the pressure," or "You look so much prettier with a smile. Why don't you smile more?" These men typically portray themselves as smart, funny, and charming, so it's hard to realize they've used this tactic on you until you go back and play the interaction over again in your head, after you've had time to wonder why you were left feeling worse after a compliment rather than better.

- **UNCONSTRUCTIVE FEEDBACK:** Constructive feedback is actionable and targeted at specific actions you can take to improve. Unconstructive feedback attacks your personality and character. The Neg might say, "You look too young to be a successful entrepreneur," or "Of course you wouldn't understand. You don't have enough experience." This can make you feel defensive, work extra hard to earn their approval, and become susceptible to emotional or physical manipulation in order to prove you deserve something.

- **"IT'S JUST A JOKE":** Say a man makes an inappropriate joke or comment. If you react accordingly, with disgust or anger, he'll knock you down by labeling you as stiff and saying something like "It's just a joke. Where's your sense of humor?" or "Lighten up, I can't say anything without you taking it too seriously." They deflect the blame, so suddenly it's your fault that you interpreted it the wrong way versus them taking any responsibility for being offensive in the first place.

The dangerous thing about negging is the idea that because it's not physical, it's not abuse. You may wonder if you're being overly sensitive or feel defensive. Make no mistake about it, that's part of the manipulation. Don't react unnecessarily to a Neg. The more you react, the more power you give him. Instead, confront it calmly and call it out to show that you are not having any of it. Simply say, "Save it, Joe. No one asked for your opinion," and move on with your work as if you've just waved off a pesky fly. Negging is a form of verbal and emotional harassment, and if you don't stop it in its tracks, it can easily escalate to other kinds of abuse.

The Mentor

He's rich, powerful, well-connected, and supposedly "a champion of women." He brags about the women he has mentored and offers to give you valuable advice . . . over drinks. Becoming the mentor is a tactic often used by older men with ulterior motives. They'll tell you about all the things they can offer you, invite you to have dinner with them, take you to nice places, impress you with their wise advice, and make loose promises to help you in any way they can to achieve your goals. Whether it's connections, advice, investment, or promotions, they will dangle the carrot so that it is always just out of reach. For you to earn the prize, he requires more meetings, more dinners, more drinks, and over time you become more and more vulnerable and dependent on him.

When a man is inviting you to events, sharing industry information, or offering you unsolicited acts of service, always question *why* he is offering you things. As a rule, never accept something that will make you indebted to a man. A friend of mine once had a mentor who offered to pay to freeze her eggs so she could focus on building her startup and not have to worry about the financial burden. As a bootstrapped entrepreneur, he knew how big of a deal it was because she had confided in him that egg freezing was something she had been actively considering but couldn't pursue because finances were tight. When she shared his offer with me, I immediately spotted the mentor's manipulation and persuaded her not to take it. This was a powerful man inserting himself into her bodily choices, and if she allowed him to pay, it would mean she would be indebted to him *for life*.

Dealing with mentors who may have ulterior motives can be tricky because even if you do call them out on it, they can fall back on "Well, I was just trying to help you" and then gaslight you into feeling guilty that you suspected them in the first place. So always ask yourself, *Does this offer make sense?* If it seems unnecessary or too generous for its own good, do not accept it. As a Bad Bitch, you can create your own opportunities, thank you very much.

The Cheater

He's the guy who has a wife and two kids in the suburbs. He comes into the city a few times a week or goes on business trips and conveniently forgets his ring at home. He looks for ass in the most inappropriate situations. He's usually already higher up the ladder and knows that he has enough power to get away with it, so he goes around the office, dropping bait—a smile, a wink, a nod of approval—feeling out the young analysts to see who bites. If you do, he makes you feel special and lures you in with attention and compliments. The cheater leverages a combination of charm and seniority to attract his targets and gain attention from young women, all to satisfy his own ego. The cheater wants to have his cake and eat it, too.

Women who fall for his advances become his collateral damage without even realizing it. When you find out about his cheating ways, he will not try to deny it. Sometimes, he will make an excuse, saying he and his wife have a special "arrangement," which gives him free rein to do whatever he wants. Other times he will outright lie and make you believe that his marriage is in trouble and he might leave her for you. Make no mistake: To the cheater, you are disposable. The moment there is any threat to his position, he will drop you like a scalding-hot potato. And if he's senior and you're junior, believe me, if one of you has to go, it's not going to be him. If you ever find yourself in a situation with an older married man at work, think twice before you respond to him in any way. Protect yourself, and don't become complicit in a situation where you—not he—will inevitably suffer the consequences.

The Asshole

This is the guy who makes no attempt to hide the fact that he is an aggressor. He's the Harvey Weinstein, Bill Cosby, or Roger Ailes of your industry. The man who has so much power and influence that everyone around him is afraid to call him out because he could ruin anyone's career and he knows it. The asshole often uses direct pressure to coerce you into a vulnerable position, and makes it clear there will be consequences for your career if you reject his advances. If he has the influence, he may threaten to block your promotion, ruin your reputation, or blackmail you if you don't abide by his rules.

The asshole feels he's invincible because he's gotten away with bad behavior so many times in the past. Even though he's got multiple marks in his file, it's clear that he won't be fired, and his industry buddies accept that's "just who he is."

One woman, an acquaintance working in a prominent financial firm, shared a story about a senior director she worked with who would rub up against younger female analysts at holiday parties. It was a well-known fact that he was harassing women, but HR willfully ignored it. In fact, not only did they ignore the problem, but they also literally hired an undercover bodyguard during those company events to keep him in check when he drank to protect *him* from getting too handsy with the interns. Assholes are dangerous not only because they are drunk on their own power, but because there are systems and people in place who continue to protect them from repercussions. If you find yourself in the presence of an asshole who is becoming inappropriate, refuse to play his game, walk away, and document the incident ASAP. Gather solid evidence, rally other women or allies to back you up, then file the HR report. This is neither the first nor the last time he will strike, so even if it doesn't get him fired right away, there will come a certain point where enough voices will force change.

FIGHT, FLIGHT, FREEZE

You now have an overview of the most common types of abusers. Unfortunately, this is still far from an exhaustive list, and bullshit can still happen when you least expect it, leaving you shocked and confused about what even happened in the first place. When your boundaries have been violated, there are three typical reactions you'll likely experience: Fight, flight, or freeze.

Fight

This is the instinct to react aggressively and comes from a natural place of anger. The thoughts that might cross your mind are: *How dare he?!* or *Who does he think he is?* The fighter in you will want to physically fend off your aggressor, hit him, slap him, shove him. The problem is, when you react in anger, it can worsen the situation and create an adverse reaction from your abuser. Aggression breeds more aggression, especially in men, so if you react to a man with physical retaliation, he may very well fight back, and that can put you in a risky if not outright dangerous situation where he often has the physical advantage. The other downside of reacting with "fight" mode is that it gives someone an easy opportunity to frame you as overly emotional, or worse. One woman I know shared a story of a time her fight reaction was triggered when a man rubbed up against her and put his hands on her at a late-night event. She shoved him off angrily, and as he fell backward, he started yelling and calling her a "crazy bitch." Despite her protests, when security came, all they saw was an angry, "crazy" woman. In the end, he was allowed to walk free, and she suffered the consequences. While it may feel empowering and justified in the moment, starting a fight can cause more pain than it's worth.

Flight

This is an avoidant reaction and often comes from fear of retaliation. When your flight reaction is triggered, you pretend that something never happened and try to avoid confronting it, thinking about it, or acknowledging it at all costs. This is a reaction that often occurs when you are in a subordinate position. Men in power who are repeat harassers count on this reaction from good girls who they know will be too afraid to do anything about their misconduct. However, avoiding or running away from an abusive experience has the adverse consequence of showing your harasser that they can get away with abusing you, and if you never deal with it, it simply makes them more confident in their ability to repeat the offense on you or on another woman down the line.

Freeze

This is what happens when you literally freeze and are incapable of reacting in any way to a violation. Your brain becomes too overwhelmed to communicate with your body, so you are stuck, frozen in fear as you process the incident. After a freeze, you may go through a series of emotions, starting with disbelief—*I can't believe that just happened*—followed by confusion—*Did that really happen?*—then helplessness—*What do I do now that this has happened?*—and, finally, self-doubt—*Who will even believe me that this happened?* The freeze can feel like a total system shutdown. It can be debilitating, upsetting, and nerve-racking, and also leaves you vulnerable to further abuse if you don't find a way to quickly recover.

Whatever your natural automatic reaction is, don't judge yourself for it. You can never predict how you will *react* to a given situation, but you can get smart about how you *respond*. Now that you are aware of the fight, flight, or freeze patterns, let's strategize how a Bad Bitch should respond.

HOW TO CALL OUT BULLSHIT

Bullshit can happen to you whether you've known someone for years, months, days, or even minutes; the perpetrator can be any gender, age, race, or background. So how do you spot the bullshit? It doesn't matter what industry or what stage of career you're in; in every situation there are power dynamics at play, and you need to know how to recognize and use them to your advantage. Often when someone is in a position of power in a given interaction, they focus attention on the other person and use "you" language like, "What's wrong with *you*?" in an attempt to disarm you so you don't notice their moves. When someone is in the subordinate position, they tend to use "I" language like "I think" or "I feel" and focus on themselves, making them susceptible to manipulation. When someone harasses you, they are effectively focusing their power on you (in a way that often feels threatening and isolating) to evoke an emotional or defensive reaction.

Don't let that happen.

Once you've recovered from the initial fight, flight, or freeze reaction, move the spotlight off yourself and put it back onto them as calmly as possible.

Redirect the attention by asking specific "you" questions:

- **"WHAT MAKES YOU THINK THIS IS APPROPRIATE?"**
  This question appeals to their lingering sense of justice and common sense (if they have any left) and forces them to reconsider their actions, or at least recognize your disapproval.
- **"WHAT IS YOUR INTENTION?"**
  If you ask this question, they will either try to defend themselves and make up an excuse, or they will pause and try to answer your question. Either way, you should consider their true intention behind their action: How does this help their ego? Does it make them feel more powerful? Does it make them feel needed? Does it make them look good? Does it make them feel special? (Certainly their intention wasn't to make you feel good, safe, or respected, was it?)
- **"WHO RAISED YOU?"**
  This is a punch in the gut as it shows you are clearly appalled and disappointed in their behavior, the way a mother would

be of a small, immature child. "But seriously, who made you believe this kind of behavior is acceptable?"

Every situation is unique, but always remember that you want to redirect the negative attention back onto them. Don't get upset, don't get defensive, don't engage in pointless arguments, don't stoop down to their level, but *do* make it clear their behavior is unacceptable.

Evaluate Your Environment

When something happens to you, it's important to consider your environment, as this will inform your strategic response as well: Are you in a public space where other people are around, or a private space where no one can help you? Are you at an event with people you know, or a random spot with strangers? Are you somewhere quiet where someone could hear you, or is it too loud and you'll get drowned out? Are you at a professional event, or a social gathering?

Making a scene in front of a big professional group that does not know you well is a gamble; it may have adverse consequences, especially if you get emotional, but in that situation, you do have witnesses. On the other hand, if you were to get confrontational in a private space where others are not around, things can get very dangerous. The ideal scenario is if you are in a public space with people you know, or witnesses who will have your back. Of course, this is not always the case. Do what you can with the resources available to you in the moment—your life and well-being come first.

A woman once told me a story about how she had been repeatedly hounded by an investor who wanted to sleep with her. Whenever they had private one-on-one meetings, she said, he'd proposition her. She would deflect his comments with an excuse and try to change the subject, because she knew she couldn't be aggressive or defensive with him in a private environment without witnesses.

One night she found herself at a large industry event with this man.

When he approached her and started to creep on her, she sighed loudly and, so everyone could hear, shouted "Okay, *fine*. I'll sleep with you." The room went dead silent, and she continued, "*But* only if you get written permission from your wife." His wife was standing right there next to him, completely appalled by her disgusting husband. Needless to say, the harassment stopped after that.

Leverage Allies

If you find yourself in a situation where you feel uncomfortable or unsafe directly confronting a harasser yourself, consider how you might find and leverage trusted allies to have your back and call out bullshit on your behalf.

Once, at an industry networking event, an older man started talking to me about his fund, then offered to buy me a drink. As I leaned forward to look at the cocktail menu, he inappropriately slipped his hand onto the small of my back. I immediately felt uncomfortable and slid away to find a different group of people. A few minutes later, he appeared out of nowhere, came up behind me, slapped my ass, said, "Here's your drink," and walked away.

I froze in total shock. But once I got out of the freeze, I moved into Bad Bitch mode and started thinking strategically. I was at a professional event and knew it would be disadvantageous to make a scene and risk being labeled "crazy." I also didn't feel comfortable directly confronting this man who was significantly larger than me, and who clearly had no sense of physical boundaries. So I decided it was time to leverage allies. I knew one of the organizers of the event and decided this was something he would want to know about. I told the organizer what had happened to me, pointed out the perpetrator, and said, "I feel extremely uncomfortable and unsafe speaking to him, so I need your help to do something about this."

The next day, the organizer told me that he had spoken to the perpetrator and had taken care of it. He made it clear that he was no longer invited to upcoming events, and I could rest assured knowing that this guy would think twice before slapping another woman's ass. This was a powerful move, because now it wasn't just me holding him accountable—it was his industry peers, who could have a real impact on his reputation and career.

Always remember, even one woman saying "enough is enough" has the power to completely change a system. When you call out bullshit, whether in person or online, you make it clear that you will not tolerate it going forward. This not only empowers you, but it also empowers the women around you to do the same. You now have the tools to stop a perpetrator in his tracks, so whether you call out bullshit directly or bring in reinforcements, make sure they know that they chose the wrong Bad Bitch to mess with.

PART THREE

BANK ACCOUNT

"A woman who imitates a man can only go as far as a man, but a woman who embraces her full feminine power is unstoppable."

—Lisa Carmen Wang

COMMANDMENT 7

A BAD BITCH LOVES MONEY

CLIPPING COUPONS

One of my earliest money memories is of clipping coupons with my mother. Every Sunday, we had an unspoken tradition: together we would sit at the kitchen table surrounded by newspapers and magazines and rummage through to find the best discounts on everything from tea to toilet paper to tennis shoes. Discovering deals felt like finding secret treasure, and by the end of our sessions, we would have stacks of nicely cut coupons ready to go.

When my mom and I went shopping, we would head straight to the clearance aisles and see if there were any steals that had been overlooked. When the time came to check out, I would pull out a fistful of coupons and proudly hand them over to the cashier. I lived for that victorious moment when the screen ceremoniously displayed the discounted price.

Like many immigrant kids, I grew up with the understanding that money was not something to waste, and carelessness was not within our means. I knew the sacrifice my parents had made to come to

America, and I saw how hard they worked to provide a good life for our family. Moreover, growing up as one of the few Asian families on the fringes of a predominately white, upper-middle-class suburb, I felt a constant pressure to prove that I could do just as well as—if not better than—my peers. Under the circumstances, I believed the road to wealth was through effort and accumulation: working twice as hard as everyone else and saving every last penny. I believed things like: *I must be frugal. I can't spend too much money. I can't be selfish. I can't ask for too much. I must be grateful for every dollar.*

These were the financial beliefs that, without consciously realizing it, would shape my relationship with money for years to come, causing me to consistently undervalue my abilities, undersell my services, and struggle to ask for more. As a good girl who was always eager to please, I had no trouble working myself ragged to earn more money, money I would then desperately hold on to.

By the time I became an entrepreneur, I readily bought into the *hustle hard, succeed at all costs* mentality that the New York and Silicon Valley startup worlds championed. In the first couple years of my business, I worked twelve hours a day, barely slept, and paid myself below minimum wage. I vividly remember once jolting awake at 3:00 a.m., my keyboard imprinted on my cheek, empty snack bags sprawled across my desk, then, without hesitation, blinking the sleep from my eyes and going straight back to work until the sun rose. In some twisted, roundabout way, I became addicted to suffering, believing that pain was a natural indicator of success. I believed the alternative was failure, and I was determined to succeed no matter the costs to my health, my sanity, or my happiness.

Luckily, my hustle didn't go to waste. My startup was acquired, and based on the headlines, everything looked great; however, despite being successful on paper, I was utterly burnt-out and numb. On the day I signed the papers for the acquisition, I looked at the woman in the mirror and struggled to recognize her; her face was covered in rashes of eczema, and her puffy eyes were shadowed with dark circles. This was not the image of a Bad Bitch who was building her empire. This was the image of a woman who had fallen back into the toxic grasp of Good Girl Brainwashing, who prioritized everything and everyone but herself, and who didn't fully believe she deserved the money she'd made or the success she'd achieved.

After spending my whole life believing that I had to suffer to prove myself "worthy," that I had to sacrifice myself to make more money, my overworked and exhausted body was telling me something had to change.

FEAR AND SHAME KEEP US POOR

For too long, women have had to apologize for wanting to be unapologetically rich and powerful. We are told that we must be generous givers, that we must be supermoms, that we must be good wives, but what are we not told? To dream of kicking ass, building empires, and making a shit ton of money. Whether by omission or outright being told, most women aren't raised to believe in our own power and potential, let alone to harness it. We aren't even allowed to say we want money in the first place for fear that others will say we're greedy or selfish. So what do we do? We continue trying to prove we deserve money, often by passive-aggressively hinting that we'd like more of it—but no worries if not.

Good Girl Brainwashing has made so many of us irrationally afraid of money—earning it, asking for it, and unapologetically believing ourselves deserving of it. When the topic of personal finances comes up, many women dismiss it. But the reality is, this dismissal is simply masking fear—fear of losing money, fear of not having enough money, fear of being judged about money. It is a self-sabotaging spiral of financial ignorance and shame that only serves to do one thing: keep us poor.

The roots of this run deep. Society socializes women to be deeply disconnected from money from a young age. Early on, girls often do not receive the same kind of exposure to money as boys do, whether through our families or through the media. The powerful effect of early financial exposure is not to be underestimated: while boys typically develop a visceral and positive connection to money—whether through emulating the primary breadwinner (traditionally their father), or through prominently featured male business and investment moguls in media like Bill Gates, Warren Buffett, Jeff Bezos, and so on—they are conditioned to see money as a tool for freedom and power. Girls, on the other hand, are often left in the dark.

This problem is widespread, cross-generational, and often exacerbated in multiple ways:

- Traditionally, fathers have been considered head of the household and controlled most financial assets. When mothers do not participate in money matters, daughters often become similarly disconnected from money and lack confidence when it comes time to manage their own finances.
- Socially, groups of girls do not often congregate to challenge, barter, gamble, or play games the same way boys do, resulting in lower risk tolerance and a lack of practice in investing and exchanging assets.
- Culturally, the media does not celebrate and feature prominent female business role models the same way it does men. On the occasions that women are featured, instead of discussing women's business prowess, the media traditionally loves to criticize them for everything from their appearance to their romantic choices. If she does make it into the spotlight for

her work as the "female CEO," god forbid she make even the slightest mistake, and have her failure be blown out of proportion to represent the failure of "all women."

• Financial education is largely created by and for an audience that is male, pale, and stale. Nearly 70 percent of all money articles targeted at men are about growing money and investing; in contrast, 90 percent of money articles targeted toward women focus on saving and spending less.

When left with inadequate or negative exposure to money, we grow up never fully understanding the value of a dollar, our own earning potential, or the power of money. For women, this lack of understanding often manifests as the internalized false belief that money is complicated and difficult, so we continue to procrastinate getting started on anything money-related—from budgeting to investing.

Because of the way I grew up, money was an ongoing source of anxiety and shame, something that I was always fighting against, something I didn't understand, something that could always slip away. As a result, I developed such a toxic relationship with money that no matter how much or how little I made, it was never enough. I was using the excuse of "I never have time" because I was "always working" to avoid facing my own shame around my lack of personal finance skills. At a certain point, I simply believed it was too late to start learning and I would sound stupid if I asked for help.

After I realized I could no longer ignore my body's unavoidable signs of burnout, I decided I had to put my ego aside and fix my relationship with money once and for all. I committed to doing the work of deeply analyzing my internal narrative around money and, in turn, focused on releasing bad habits that no longer served me. I took a long, hard look at my income and expenses and mapped out my long-term financial goals. I even invested in a financial coach to keep me on track and accountable. I'm not going to lie: transforming my relationship with money challenged me constantly. Going from a scarcity mindset to an abundance mindset, from fear to love of money, felt extremely unnatural, but what I discovered through that process changed everything. I realized that when you are afraid of not having enough money, you don't own it—it owns *you*. You become a slave to the fear, so you don't invest, you don't budget, and you don't spend wisely.

When you love money, you are not afraid to unapologetically say "I want money" and "I deserve money." When you put this abundant energy out into the world, there is no limit to the wealth you can tap into. Like love, money becomes an endlessly renewable resource that every Bad Bitch can access. All it takes is the courage to admit you want it and deserve to have it.

FINANCIAL FICTIONS

Imagine your relationship with money like you would a relationship with a person. In a healthy, loving relationship, you nurture and help each other grow. You pay attention to the small details and communicate what you need because you care about the other person and the success of the relationship. In a toxic relationship, you might cling or try to control them, refusing to let them out of your sight for fear that they might leave you. Or you might be the hot-and-cold type— one day you're texting the other person constantly, and the next day you're radio silent and completely avoiding them.

Now compare those extremes with your relationship with money. Do you pay close attention to your bank statements? Or do you spend recklessly one day and then avoid checking your bills the next? Are you investing and helping your money grow, or are you holding on to it and suffocating it in a savings account? Be honest with yourself: When it comes to your relationship with money, are you really showing up as your best self, and can you trust that you can and will achieve abundance?

If you are in any way dissatisfied with your current financial situation, it means that there is room for improvement. Like any relationship, we each bring our fair share of baggage, and it's no different with money. All of us carry around what I call "Financial Fictions" in our heads that dictate how we think about money, how we interact with it, and how it makes us feel—and these narratives take root a lot earlier in life than we think. A Financial Fiction is a false story we tell ourselves about money that makes us fear, disdain, or reject the abundance it could bring into our lives. Almost all the women I've coached over the years have Financial Fictions that hold them back from fulfilling their full potential.

One of those women, Alina—an immigrant and the only English speaker in her family—was put in charge of her family's finances at a young age and was forced to learn how to save and stretch every dollar to the penny. Eventually, she was able to get a full ride to college, and once there, her hard work earned her paid grants to study abroad. She fell in love with traveling in developing countries and would tell me stories about how cheap everything was and how she could buy so much with so little. After another one of her trips, this time to Southeast Asia, she came back and excitedly told me about a digital nomad who had mastered the cheap backpacker lifestyle: traveling the world and surviving by doing odd jobs online. "See, you really don't need that much money to have a great life," she told me excitedly.

While what she said is true, I knew that Alina's Bad Bitch Dream was to one day launch a global education startup, so scraping by to survive as an itinerant backpacker seemed inconsistent with her larger goals. When I asked her about this, she got defensive. "Of course I know I could make more money, but I know plenty of rich people who are spoiled and miserable, and I don't ever want to be like that," she explained, scrunching her nose up like the words themselves smelled bad.

And there it was, Alina's Financial Fiction: "Too much money corrupts people, and I'm better off without it." In her mind, she conflated being "rich" with being "spoiled, greedy, and unhappy" on the one hand, and being "financially modest" with being "resourceful, hardworking, and satisfied" on the other. Her overall beliefs were too black-and-white, and without consciously realizing it, these beliefs were holding her back from achieving her dreams. When we dug further into her Financial Fiction, she realized that deep down, it wasn't that she didn't want to make more money—she was terrified of admitting that she wanted *more*. Having grown up lower-middle-class, a part of her felt guilty for desiring more than her family ever had. Simultaneously, she was hesitant to set bigger financial goals for fear that she might fail.

In Alina's case, we had to realign her perception of money as a tool for freedom and impact. To do this, however, she had to make some critical money mindset shifts, from "I don't need money" to "I deserve money," from "money corrupts" to "money empowers," from "money is wasteful" to "money is impactful."

I asked Alina, "What could more money help you achieve, personally?" Instead of focusing on her fear of failing, we envisioned how empowering it would feel to reach her goals. To her, financial independence meant enabling a life where she could travel as she pleased, buy her own property, fund the launch of her business, and eventually start a family—all things she genuinely believed she deserved to have.

Next, I asked her, "What impact could you make with more money?" She talked about one day building schools in developing countries and admitted that more money would allow her to create programs to educate more children who otherwise wouldn't have access to a quality education. By zooming out on her bigger goals and pinpointing her desire to help others less fortunate than her, she was able to see that money could be a powerful tool for change when leveraged intentionally, especially by people like herself. It took rewriting all these Financial Fictions before Alina finally felt not only comfortable, but excited to start taking charge of her bank account.

Your Financial Fiction

While it may seem daunting to dig into your past and extricate all the hidden influences that may be shaping your relationship with money, this is a crucial—and often the most overlooked—step every woman must take to move forward and start taking charge of her finances.

No matter what income bracket you were raised in, limiting beliefs around money can develop in any household. Just like we didn't choose our parents or where we were born, we also didn't have a choice in the beliefs we absorbed as children. As adults, however, we can decide to break the cycle.

The first step in releasing any negative influence from your life is to become aware of its existence. Cultivating awareness about the subconscious narratives that negatively impact our lives is one of the most important skills for personal growth. Over the next few pages, you'll have the opportunity to bring awareness to your Financial Fiction through a series of writing prompts.

As you respond to the following prompts, don't think too hard about your answers or censor yourself. These exercises are designed to elicit a gut reaction, so follow your intuition and let your thoughts flow without judgment. It may be difficult, even painful to dig into your past and find skeletons in closets you didn't even know were there. Be kind to yourself and remember that discomfort is a necessary part of growth and change.

Note: Don't just think about your answers; write them down. When you put things in writing, you can see the challenges in front of you more clearly. Only when you make your Financial Fictions tangible do you have a fighting chance of releasing their hold on you once and for all. Take out a pen and answer the following:

My earliest memory of money was . . .

_____

_____

My father's relationship with money was . . .

_____

_____

My mother's relationship with money was . . .

_____

_____

As a result, I grew up believing that money was . . .

_____

_____

There's a reason why Financial Fictions have so much power and influence over us. Our earliest beliefs often create patterns of behavior, and these patterns give us a sense of comfort because we see and experience them as "just the way things are." This is how people like Alina grow up to think of having money as inherently greedy. We become accustomed to our own idea of "normal" and subconsciously craft a narrative to support it, even if that narrative is harmful to us.

When we get used to the feeling of financial shame in childhood, we continue to act in ways that give power to this feeling, allowing it to build via our bad habits. Every time we undervalue ourselves, every time we avoid investing, every time we provide free labor, we are only giving more credence to our Financial Fictions.

Now think about how your Financial Fiction continues to affect you in the present:

My greatest limiting belief that prevents me from making more money is . . .

_____

This limiting belief shows up in the form of repetitive negative thoughts like . . .

_____

This limiting belief shows up in the form of self-sabotaging behaviors and habits like . . .

_____

Read back what you just wrote, and ask yourself: *Is this the belief you still want to live by? Are these thoughts and habits you want to hold on to? What are you doing or not doing that you know you need to change? What are the consequences of not changing?*

Very often, all it takes to free yourself from your Financial Fiction is to take that first small step—whether that's deciding to log in to your bank account to view last month's statements, putting an event on your calendar to review your weekly expenses, or learning about how taxes work. Imagine how good it will feel when you finally take over the reins from your Financial Fiction once and for all.

The first step I will take to release my Financial Fiction will be . . .

_____

When I release my Financial Fiction, I will feel . . .

_____

Taking charge of your relationship with money now will have a huge impact not only on how you feel but also on how much you make in the future. Think about it this way: Money is energy. It is neither inherently positive or negative, but the way you feel about it can give it a positive or negative charge. You can thoughtfully exchange it for something that brings you joy, or you can impulsively spend it on something that brings you regret. Whatever energy you put out, you attract. If you're serious about changing your financial narrative, focus on putting out positive and loving energy toward money so you can attract it back to you.

I love money because it enables me to . . .

_____

I deserve money because I am . . .

_____

Turn these answers into your money mantra and continue to cultivate a positive outlook toward your finances. Do you see how much of a difference it can make when you believe to your core that money is a source of positivity and power? There is no reason you need to be shackled by your Financial Fiction any longer. By facing your fears head-on and taking the necessary action to reverse them, you are bringing transparency to your money habits and ultimately creating a sustainable path toward that beautiful place known as financial independence.

MONEY ON YOUR OWN TERMS

While there is no set definition for "financial independence," in the context of being a Bad Bitch, "financial independence" means having the money to live the life *you want*, on *your terms*, on *your dime* . . . and with money left over to silence the haters (aka "fuck-you money"). It doesn't matter where you are in your career, or what industry you are in, understanding yourself financially and creating a strategy that builds toward financial independence is paramount.

To this day, a staggering 56 percent of married women leave investment and long-term financial planning decisions to their husbands, and 85 percent of women who do this believe their spouses know more about finances than them. But what happens when things go south? Divorce, separation, or death of a partner can leave women blindsided and drowning in debt. Financial infidelity—having a secret bank account or credit card, concealing significant debt, hiding an expensive purchase—is more common than you think. Even if you are married to a seemingly amazing partner who loves managing the household finances, the fact that 70 percent of women fire their male advisors within a year of their spouse's death, and 90 percent will hire a female advisor after, shows that you can't assume that your partner's advice is always in your best interest. While there may always be situations that are out of your control, to the extent that you have the ability, you never want to purposely put yourself in a position where you need to beg someone for money to live your life. Without direct access to your own bank account, you are fully at the mercy of someone else, and a Bad Bitch can't afford that. You need to be able to stand on your own two feet so that no matter if you end a relationship or you're fired, you can always take care of yourself.

Something all financially independent Bad Bitches have in common? We think long term. Regardless of your current income level, long-term thinking is a critical factor in accumulating wealth, and it starts with defining your individual financial and lifestyle goals. What kind of life do you want to live? Where do you want to be in one year? Five? Ten? What do you want to own? What do you want to never have to worry about? There is no right or wrong answer to any of these questions, but the process starts with clearly defining your long-term goals and mapping out the money milestones necessary to achieve them.

I recommend starting with stating your goals, unapologetically. Sky's the limit for how big you can go. For example, after one of my mentees, Tess, finished grad school, she stated that her long-term goals included: owning her own apartment in New York City, buying her parents a house by the beach, and being able to fly business class whenever her heart desired.

Tess was aware that these were lofty goals, and money wasn't going to just fall from the sky. If she wanted to achieve this lifestyle, she would need to be disciplined in everything from budgeting to investing to choosing the industry she worked in. The first steps she took included: taking an inventory of her bank account's assets and liabilities, opening a high-yield savings account, maxing out her retirement accounts, and committing a percentage of her paycheck into her investment budget each month so that her money was working for her, on top of her regular salary. Finally, she made a long-term strategic decision to pursue a career in tech, knowing that this was a growing industry that boasted some of the highest salaries and bonuses in the country. Tess took charge of her financial future by clearly stating her long-term goals, reverse engineering a plan with specific milestones, *and* taking action to consistently grow her money. Today, Tess is well on her way to achieving her Bad Bitch Dream of financial independence.

BAD BITCH MONEY MOVES

Everyone's money goals are different. Regardless of how modest or how grand yours are, there are a few basic money moves every Bad Bitch should make to get your finances straight. Set these things up properly and they will save you immense amounts of time and suffering down the line so you can focus on the things that really matter. Think of it like going to the dentist. You might dread it, but you know that it's for your own good. So take it as a necessary evil and pat yourself on the back when you get your financial foundations in place.

Track Your Expenses

Knowledge is power. Knowing what you spend money on and what your nonnegotiables are, and then cutting out unnecessary short-term expenses, is key to long-term financial independence. An easy way to start doing this is by taking inventory of what you spend money on over the course of a couple weeks. Notice the trends: Are you spending a lot more than you'd like on eating out? On online purchases? On unused subscriptions? Tess, for example, noticed that she was eating out a lot, but it wasn't the food that was costing her, it was the Ubers home afterward. She decided that dinners with her friends were nonnegotiable because they brought her so much joy, so she came up with a couple solutions: Once a week, she scheduled dinners out earlier in the evening so she could have the option of taking public transit home at a decent hour. She also started inviting her friends over for home-cooked meals so she could enjoy their company at a fraction of the cost. She saved several hundred dollars a month just by being intentional about the details, and that extra savings gave her what she needed to start building up her investment accounts.

Max Out Your Retirement Accounts

Retirement may seem like a lifetime away, but for many of us, making contributions to a tax-deferred 401(k) and/or Roth IRA today is the single biggest and easiest way to lower your tax liability and passively build wealth long term. These types of accounts are tax-deferred, meaning you can allow your money to compound tax-free until you withdraw it down the line. To put it in tangible terms, if you started contributing $500 per month to your Roth IRA at 25 years old with an 8 percent annual return, by the time you're 65, you will have over $1.5 million in the bank and over $600K in tax savings. Want to see the exponential growth yourself? Find an online Roth IRA calculator and plug in the numbers to see how much you could be making. There's no excuse not to start—you can by easily opening an account with most online brokers.

Automate Investing

When you don't invest, you literally lose money every day due to inflation. And there is no better generator of long-term wealth than investing, due to the magic of compound interest. To put it into context, if you invest $1,000 monthly starting today, it can grow to over $5 million in fifty years at a 7 percent annual interest rate because interest from your investments begins to generate its own interest, creating an exponentially profitable snowball effect. That's not chump change. So how do you dip your toe in? The average Bad Bitch is busy and doesn't have time to individually hand-pick stocks, so the best way to get into the market is through an exchange-traded fund (ETF) so you can hold a basket of diversified stocks. In the past, you needed a large sum of money and an expensive financial advisor to help you open up a brokerage account and make investments, but now, with the help of technology, getting started in the stock market has never been easier or cheaper. Moreover, robo-advisors are software platforms that use algorithms to automatically invest on your behalf. They take into account your goals, your risk profile, and your timeline to invest in a diversified portfolio of investments for you. The rule of thumb is to allocate 10–20 percent of your monthly budget into your investment portfolio and invest a certain amount of money on a regular weekly or monthly basis—a strategy called dollar-cost averaging—to maximize your time and return on investment. When it comes to your automated investments, there's no need to check in more than once a quarter. The markets are constantly moving, but if you're consistently putting money in, your long-term investments will accumulate and grow over time.

Stay Focused

As you start making more money, it is easy to fall into the trap of comparing yourself to others and constantly wanting more. Social media gives us the impression that everyone we see online is richer and happier than they really are. The reality is, sometimes the people who are the loudest about showing off their material wealth are barely scraping by or have terrible money management skills. Point being, there is no need to feel inadequate when you see others making more or flaunting what you might assume is their wealth. Stay focused on your own goals, be forgiving of your mistakes, and celebrate yourself for reaching your own money milestones on your path toward financial independence.

Invest in Your Most Valuable Asset

At the end of the day, loving money means loving yourself. No matter where you are in your financial journey, you are your most valuable asset, and as such you must be your first and most intentional investment. That means investing in anything that facilitates your personal or professional growth: courses, training, or coaching. This can also include investing in your business or brand, hiring personnel, or creating IP. If you have any lingering fears about losing money, investing in yourself is the fastest way to get over it. Why? Because when you invest in yourself, you make your skills and experience more valuable. The more valuable you are, the more confident you become in your ability to make money.

So long as you are confident in your ability to make money, you will never fear being without it. I once invested $2,000 in an online course to learn how to build and sell my own $2,000 online course.

There were several hundred people on the free webinar, and all of them wanted to turn their expertise into a paid course, but the majority stated they "could not afford to spend $2,000 up front" and dropped out. However, as the teacher rightfully said, "This is an investment in yourself. If you believe you can get one customer, then your investment will have paid itself back."

Did I believe I could get at least one paying customer? Yes. Did I believe I had something valuable to teach? Hell yes. One of the financial goals I had set early on as an entrepreneur was to learn how to make six figures in passive income online, and this was a perfect way to do so. I believed in myself, so I made the $2,000 investment. Within six months, I made over $200,000 in course sales from the knowledge I gained from that one class. That's a nearly 100x return, my greatest return on investment to date. At the end of the day, a Bad Bitch is always willing to invest in her most valuable asset: herself.

Sometimes I think back to that coupon-clipping good girl I once was and get an adrenaline rush, knowing just how far she's come. Who knew that one day she would achieve the financial independence she had always dreamed of and enjoy the journey on top of it? No matter how you define financial independence, make sure it feels good for you. Your goals and budget will evolve over time; that is perfectly normal. Financial independence is an iterative process of learning, investing, and growing. That being said, I encourage you to have fun along the way. When making money becomes positive and pleasurable, a Bad Bitch is always down to play.

COMMANDMENT 8

A BAD BITCH COMMANDS HER WORTH

THE GOOD GIRL DISCOUNT

"How much do you charge?" I asked.

I was on a Zoom call with a man who had recently left his startup job to launch his own independent coaching business.

"My prices start at $15,000 and go up to $100,000 for my annual clients," he stated matter-of-factly.

I stared at him dumbfounded. "Are you serious?" I was charging a fraction of what he had been charging, even though I objectively had more experience than he did. When I told him my pricing, it was his turn to stare at me dumbfounded.

"Are *you* serious?" he echoed. "Why are you charging so low?"

It was a valid question. By the time I launched my independent coaching practice, I had built and sold a startup that supported over twenty thousand female entrepreneurs and facilitated tens of millions in funding for female-led businesses. Having spent over ten thousand hours researching, analyzing, and helping women in building their confidence and nailing their pitches, I was undoubtedly an expert in coaching my core demographic; however, when it came time for me to set my own prices, I was clearly not immune to the good girl tendency to undervalue and discount myself.

I tried to rationalize my lower prices to him and explained, "Well, my clients just aren't able to pay that much for coaching." In my experience, many women would push back and ask for discounts for coaching, and I would gladly oblige because I felt bad for charging more than they could afford.

"But I have female clients, and they are also willing to pay my prices," he countered. "I don't think it's about gender. Anyone can pay if they really want your services."

Perhaps he was right. Was I just making up excuses for why I couldn't charge more? After I hung up and started retooling my pricing model, my automatic instinct still was to take the low end of his pricing bracket and cut it in half. But I immediately caught myself and wondered, *What in the world am I doing?*

When I was first getting my startup off the ground, I had paid $12,000 for my first business coach despite being extremely strapped for cash at the time. My rationale? All the greatest entrepreneurs I knew had business coaches, and every single one of them told me it was one of the best investments they made, so I found a way to pay for one myself. Once I invested and committed to the process, the results were tremendous. Coaching delivered the mental and financial results that helped me thrive through the toughest times as I built my company. But even though I had personally experienced the value of coaching, and even though I had built up my own coaching expertise, I was still so reluctant to charge more when it came time to value my own services.

As I dug in, I realized I simply didn't believe I was worthy of being paid as a high-priced coach. Despite having a wealth of relevant experience, I felt ashamed to charge more because I wanted to see myself as a woman driven by impact and purpose, and not as a "greedy" businesswoman. I succumbed to the false dichotomy that purpose and profit could not coexist. The result? I sacrificed the profit. I continued discounting myself and taking on more and more clients to try and earn the amount of money I had set out to make.

While this seemed harmless enough at first, over time it began to take its toll. I started to feel overworked and undervalued as I discovered that my lower-paying clients were also clearly less invested in the work. The worst part was realizing that the work I had initially loved so much had become a source of resentment.

PAID IN PENNIES

Women today are earning 60 percent of undergraduate and graduate degrees, and for the first time, women comprise the majority of the college-educated workforce. What's more, women of color are leading the way and enrolling at record rates, with Latina women comprising the biggest increase in employment of any working group and Black women following closely behind. Clearly, the old excuse that there "aren't enough qualified women in the pipeline" is a total cop-out.

With so many educated women getting down to work, why are we still getting paid less? The fact is, no matter how much positive press there is hyping up women at the lowest ranks, nothing will change until we acknowledge that men are way overrepresented in the highest-paid decision-making roles, and this inordinately affects how businesses are run and the types of people who rise. Although educated women and men are hired at equal rates, women are not promoted or paid at the same rate. Only twenty-four of the Fortune 500 companies are led by women, and almost all are white. While this is the most women ever at the helm of our biggest organizations, that's still less than 5 percent overall. The biggest drop-off point for women is the VP level—when we have the greatest leverage, but also when we encounter the greatest amount of bias and politics that keep us from rising into true positions of power. Employers often implicitly punish women at this stage in life if there is any indication that she may start prioritizing a family by questioning her "commitment" to the company. Even if she is given more responsibility or vanity title bumps, compensation often continues to lag behind that of male counterparts.

No doubt, there are many things working against us—from ignorant comments to outright stupidity—but how are *we* complicit in perpetuating this pay gap? Research shows that 60 percent of women never negotiate their first salary, and 55 percent of women lower their prices before the client even asks. Have we simply gotten used to getting paid less? Have we been Good Girl Brainwashed to feel grateful for getting paid pennies? In short, yes. So many of the women I work with tell me they feel grateful for getting the opportunity to be in their current roles, especially if they come from lower-income families and defied the odds to get a high-paying job in fields like law, consulting, tech, or finance. Many are already making more than they ever imagined, and don't want to risk coming off greedy, much less getting fired, if they ask for more. Good girls love to underpromise and overdeliver. So instead of commanding their worth, asking for more, and leveraging up to get paid and promoted, many good girls focus on doing the same thing that got them in the door in the first place—doing a good job.

For female entrepreneurs, there is a similar phenomenon. Because so few of us receive funding, we ask for less and are grateful to receive anything at all. Men not only close more checks, but they also close greater amounts simply because they believe they are worth more, a belief heavily reinforced by our patriarchal society. On average, female entrepreneurs ask for roughly $35,000 less in business financing than men. Unsurprisingly, those same entrepreneurs receive significantly less as a result.

Every time women ask me for tips on fundraising, I joke that they must "Walk into the room with the confidence of a mediocre white man," and sadly, they all get it immediately. When I asked male entrepreneurs who had raised tens of millions of dollars for advice on how to secure money from investors, they told me, "Sell the dream and create FOMO. Just fake it until you make it. Make everyone think they're missing out if they don't get in on the deal."

This method is effective to an extent. But what the men who told me that failed to recognize was that their advice carried an automatic sense of entitled confidence and self-worth that assumed success. Moreover, male and female entrepreneurs get asked different questions by investors—and it affects how much funding they get. In typical investor meetings, 66 percent of the questions directed toward male entrepreneurs were focused on future potential—questions like, "What is your vision for the future of your company?" Whereas 66 percent of the questions directed toward female entrepreneurs were scrutinizing their experience: "How will you compete as a first-time CEO if your competitor has more money and more experience than you?" Men are put in positions where they are given the benefit of the doubt, and women are put in positions where we must prove we are worthy of being in the room and getting any money in the first place.

While there are certainly many things working against us, there's a point at which we need to say "enough is enough" and take matters into our own hands. Your hard work might have gotten you in the door, but what gets you to the next level is asserting your value and commanding your worth in dollars. The reality is, until we start asking for more and refusing to settle for less, we will continue to scrape by on whatever's leftover from the men at the top.

ASSERT YOUR VALUE

Before you can make more money, you need to believe in the deepest part of your subconscious that you are worth more money. Past a certain threshold, I wholeheartedly believe that the people who make more money are not necessarily better or smarter than you or me, they simply have the know-how to charge more for their time. Note I didn't say the "courage" to charge more money, as women who have been underpaid often think that asking for more money is something we muster the courage to do. The man next to you might be making more money not because he was more courageous, but simply because he was socialized to believe he was worth more, he didn't second-guess his ask, and he was more willing to walk away if he believed he was being paid below his worth.

This is the exact place I want you to reach as a negotiator: to be so secure in your sense of self-worth that you could spot a lowball offer from a mile away and walk away from it without a second thought.

Laura, an immigrant from Taiwan, grew up pinching pennies, and when she came to the US, she worked tirelessly to get into a top private university; focused and determined, she went on to land a prestigious product manager role in Silicon Valley a couple years after graduation. In her job interview, she initially proposed a $100,000 salary to her hiring manager and was blown away when she ended up receiving $120,000 in her final offer. The amount was unfathomable to her, more than anyone in her family had ever made. She was thrilled, until she realized that everyone else in her position was making $150,000.

She was so grateful for the opportunity that when the hiring manager asked about her salary expectations, she had named an amount she would accept instead of asking what the job itself paid. Most likely, the budgeted range for the role was between $120–$150K/year, so she ended up receiving the bare minimum.

Her mistake? She didn't come in with a high-enough benchmark.

Her own subjective belief in her lower worth was skewed because she was benchmarking against her past and not to the present.

On a tactical level, what she should have done was arm herself with the market data so she knew what to expect based on her role, industry, company size, and location. Then, when the hiring manager asked her salary expectations, she should have pushed back and made sure she had enough information to propose a number that made the most sense.

On a personal level, she needed to do the work to unapologetically embrace her self-worth. Like many good girls, her overwhelming gratitude overrode her ability to properly assert her value and own the experiences and skills that got her the opportunity in the first place.

COUNTER THE FIRST OFFER

In negotiation coaching, women ask me tactical questions like, "Who should go first?" "Should I negotiate over email?" "How many times should I go back and forth with the offer?" Truth is, there is no specific play that works every time because every single negotiation is unique.

The fundamental thing to understand is that it doesn't matter how many tactics you learn, you will not succeed if you struggle with low self-worth. Go in mentally prepared to command what you deserve, and *never* make the mistake of prematurely lowballing yourself when someone could have paid you more.

So how do you ensure this? By going into full-blown investigation mode. Before entering into any negotiation, you must be fully prepared. Not only do you want to understand industry benchmarks, you want to know exactly who and what you will be dealing with. When dealing with a company, research the following:

- **WHAT IS THE CURRENT FINANCIAL SITUATION OF THE COMPANY?** Have they raised a lot of money recently? Are they having a profitable year? Positive financial indicators like these mean they likely have a plush budget you can play with.
- **WHAT IS THE COMPENSATION CULTURE LIKE?** Do they treat and pay women at the company fairly? Do they tend to pay above, below, or at the market rate? Do your own background checks and try to speak directly with women at the company to understand their take on company culture and compensation.
- **WHAT KIND OF ADDITIONAL INCENTIVES DO THEY OFFER?** Do they provide value to employees in the form of equity, paid time off, or something else? Sometimes companies may be very generous with alternative compensation as a way to add additional padding. Understand the value of these, but make sure you still get paid accordingly in cold, hard cash.
- **IS THERE A PRECEDENT FOR YOUR ROLE?** Or is this the first time they are paying for something like this? If the latter, this may be your chance to really flex your value and set a high-budget precedent.

The same line of questioning applies if you are an entrepreneur negotiating with individual clients or customers: be aware of their financial position, their cultural conditioning when it comes to money (in other words, are they cheap or generous?), and any other incentives that can add value for both parties.

One additional piece of research is to ask other Bad Bitches in your industry how they are pricing themselves. Time for some solidarity and salary transparency. By asking, you save valuable time and guesswork, and a Bad Bitch is always open to sharing her best practices. While you don't have to charge the exact same amount your peers charge, it gives you a foundation to build up from.

When you've done your due diligence, you can confidently go

into any deal prepared to ask smart questions and discuss the first offer.

If you are asked to propose the first offer, always ask, "What range do you have budgeted for this project/role?" Listen closely to how they respond to this question. Depending on how strict or how lax they are with the range, you will know how high you can push the boundaries of their budget.

Other times, the employer or client is the one who throws out the first offer. In this case, no matter what you do, never accept the first offer you are given. This applies whether you are given a job offer, a consulting offer, or an investment offer. There is *always* room to negotiate. The first offer is almost never the best offer anyone can give you. Unless you are entering into a negotiation with someone who is completely broke (in which case, bitch, *run!*), it is important to at least ask and see what options are available.

When people present their first offer, they expect that the other party will negotiate. If they give you a low offer, it's not necessarily because they don't value you, but because they have built-in wiggle room, expecting that you will push back. Counter with questions to understand what value they are expecting with their offer. You can ask, "What does success look like to you?" "Why are you most interested in working with me?" You are simply gathering information to better understand if your expectations are aligned. Remember you are being considered for a role because people see your skills and experience as valuable and, as such, you should be paid accordingly if they want to get your best work. Once you've collected more information, matter-of-factly give your counteroffer.

Sometimes women will tell me that they don't want to push back because they're afraid the other party won't like them. I want to reiterate that there is absolutely nothing shameful or greedy about asking for more. This is part of the game, so if you don't ask, you are automatically leaving money on the table. A Bad Bitch who commands her worth sees the first offer as merely a starting point, and her automatic reflex is to see if she can bump it up 20 percent.

Don't get it twisted: this doesn't mean that getting more is as easy as asking for it. It just means there is always room to do so. Knowing this, see it as part of the process and be willing to counter. It's as simple as stating, "Let me know if it's feasible to do $XYZ. I'm excited to work with you and want to make it a win-win for both of us."

Remember, when you counter the first offer, you not only open up the possibility of receiving an even sweeter deal, you showcase that you place a high value on your time and services, and by extension, the other party would be lucky to have the opportunity to work with you.

When it comes to deciding on an offer, never feel pressured to accept or reject right on the spot. Beware of people who create false urgency by forcing you to decide before you're ready. If you feel uncomfortably pressured, listen to the feeling: that is most likely not the offer you want to accept. You have the right to ask for more time. When you really make time and space to listen to yourself, your body will always tell you if an offer feels good. If you sense that someone is applying false urgency, graciously thank them for the offer, and tell them you will give them a decision in twenty-four hours. Of course, the best-case scenario is if you're able to flip the pressure around so it is in your favor. You achieve this by doing the work beforehand to secure multiple offers so you can come to the table ready with evidence that you are in high demand and will only seriously consider the best offer. Optionality is power.

Remember, negotiations are not binary—they aren't either successes or failures—they are conversations about exchanging value, and it is in both parties' interests to land a win-win. If you are at the table, that means someone sees value in what you bring to it. It also means that person has a vested interest in making you feel satisfied with the deal you're being offered, because the last thing anyone wants is a lose-lose deal where they get shitty work and you feel resentful. A win-win is when you are paid your true worth, and as a result feel motivated to do and deliver great work that makes the client, the boss, or the company happy with their decision to hire you.

BAD BITCH BENCHMARK

When I first started offering my consulting services, I continued telling myself the story that I wasn't "experienced enough," so I should charge less. The reality is, the price I set was not a reflection of the true value of my services—it was a reflection of my lack of confidence. Instead of owning my track record—one that clearly indicated a pattern of going above and beyond—I focused on the fact that I hadn't yet landed bigger clients, or that I hadn't made enough revenue yet, or any other excuse I could think of to diminish myself. The result? On prospective client calls, I exuded insecure good girl energy, and that attracted certain types of clients, namely people who didn't have the money to invest in growing themselves or their businesses.

Here's the reality: People don't pay you for what you do, they pay you for how much you are worth *to them*. People are paying you to solve their problems, and if they believe they'd be hard-pressed to find someone as good as you to solve that problem, then your services are invaluable, and the sky's the limit for how much you can charge for them.

Which begs the question, how do you know what you're worth in terms of actual dollars and cents? Whether you are an entrepreneur or an employee, you need to be armed with a Bad Bitch Benchmark. This is a rule of thumb you can use so you can go into negotiations confident in a rate that is commensurate with the Bad Bitch you are.

To calculate your Bad Bitch Benchmark, start by naming your hourly rate. How much would you currently charge someone per hour for your services, expertise, and advice? Got it? Okay, great, now assuming you, like most women, have been paid less than you're worth, then I want you to take that hourly rate and double it. You heard me: *double it.*

If you thought your hourly rate was $50/hour, your true hourly rate is $100/hour. If you thought your hourly rate was $250/hour, your true hourly rate is $500/hour. If you have years of industry experience and real outcomes to show for your work and currently anchor your hourly rate at $500/hour, your true hourly rate is a fat and juicy $1,000/hour. You get the gist. Use this tactic to raise your rates at your next negotiation; if you've ever accepted an offer without countering and allowed someone else to set your prices, I guarantee you have not been getting paid what you're truly worth.

You might be thinking, *That's insane. People will think I'm ridiculous if I quote that.* Here's the thing: You don't need to state your hourly rate explicitly. As an entrepreneur there is no right or wrong answer for how much you can charge. You can use your Bad Bitch Benchmark to create a bundle of services that deliver the exact outcome the client desires, but where the pricing cannot be directly attributed to the number of hours worked.

For example, in one of my negotiations, a tech company asked me to share my rate for consulting on a new media project. The thing is, they didn't have a precedent for benchmarking the kinds of services I provided, so the pricing was subjective. When I asked the client if he had a budget in mind, he told me that he hadn't really thought about it, and if I could throw him some numbers, then he could see if he could work it within his budget. By that point, I already had nearly a decade of experience, and my hourly rate was $500, so my initial instinct was to ask for that; however, following the Bad Bitch Benchmark, I challenged myself to bump it up to $1,000 per hour. Knowing that it would take me approximately ten hours per month to do the work, I pitched a $10,000-per-month package.

The package itself made no mention of the hourly rate or the number of hours worked, but rather, focused on the specific deliverables the client would find the most value in. I had done my research, so I knew that they needed someone with my expertise. They would be hard-pressed to find someone of my caliber to deliver the same quality results as consistently as I could. So, instead of pricing my offer based on my past, I priced it according to what my services were worth to the client. I was fully confident that I could deliver everything included in my proposal and had no difficulty going into the negotiation ready to command my worth and close the deal. I confidently shared the deliverables then presented my price without wavering. Did the client ultimately go for it? You bet they did. By the end of the day, I got that signature on the dotted line.

The next time you go into a negotiation, make sure to have your Bad Bitch Benchmark burned into your mind and commit that you will not discount yourself under any circumstances. Instead of accepting a lower fee for your services, reframe it and ask yourself, *How do I increase the value of my offer so it's a no-brainer to say yes?* Then be prepared to showcase how your skills and expertise are indispensable for the client and leave no question in their mind that you are the Baddest Bitch for the job.

Remember, they're not paying you for the hours, they're paying you for the outcome. And no, none of those benchmarks are "too expensive," they just can't afford you.

GET CREATIVE WITH COMP

Sometimes you might really want a job that simply can't meet your Bad Bitch Benchmark and want to make an exception. Maybe there's an impressive client you want to add to your portfolio, maybe you are considering a role at a company with a great reputation, maybe there's a job in an area you want to get more experience in so you can springboard your career, or maybe you just want to make some quick cash.

If you're in a position where you've pitched your price and the client or company says they absolutely can't budge on budget, you can get creative to find alternative ways to gain value outside of money.

For example, I often get approached to speak at conferences, but if it's a smaller company, then their budget is often below my benchmark. In these instances, if I believe it's a valuable opportunity, I will negotiate with them to find a win-win. I still tell them my original speaking fee, but then give them the opportunity to work within their budget and come up with alternative forms of compensation. Usually, I'll ask for these four things:

- **REFERRALS:** As a speaker, it's important to find new speaking opportunities. Direct referrals to other companies or conference organizers that need speakers are by far the best source of leads.
- **MARKETING:** Share your offer in the client's newsletter or social media channels as a way to promote your company or capture new business.
- **TESTIMONIALS:** Testimonials give you street cred and show other people you can be trusted. Get as many of these as you can.
- **TRAVEL AND FOOD:** Some gigs don't offer to pay you for travel, food, and hotel, so I always ask for this as a baseline, because if they're already paying me, they should at least cover the basics.

If you are applying for a job and considering an opportunity as an employee there are other factors you can negotiate that can create just as much, if not more, value to your bottom line. As an employee, you can consider negotiating to get more of the following:

- **EQUITY:** Especially if you are interviewing for a job at a high-growth startup, equity has long-term value that can be significantly more valuable if the company takes off.
- **PERSONAL DEVELOPMENT BUDGET:** Most companies have a personal development budget that employees can spend on education, coaching, or other areas of personal growth. It is to both their benefit and yours that you have as many opportunities as possible to grow as a leader.
- **VACATION DAYS:** Use them and don't lose them. You deserve a break, so inquire about the company's vacation policy and make sure you have time to recharge.
- **TEAM BUDGET:** If you are going into a management role, ask about the team you'll have around you. As you grow in the role and show you are doing a great job, there will be room down the road to ask for a larger budget to support you and the growth of the team.
- **TITLE PROMOTION:** Make sure that both your title *and* compensation adequately reflect the roles and responsibilities that you hold. Don't fall into the trap of just accepting vanity titles. If you get a title bump, make sure that it's always followed with an appropriate compensation bump as well.

When I started consulting clients on branding and marketing, I received the opportunity to work with my first crypto company. After I pitched my Bad Bitch Benchmark, the all-male team countered with half of my asking price, stating that it was the absolute maximum they were able to offer. Because I was just breaking into the industry—and also wanted some quick cash—I made an exception and was willing to take it. My priority at that point was to maximize my learning and get my first crypto client under my belt so I could unlock other clients in that industry. I decided it was worth it to add that client to my portfolio. I found out later that had I not stated my

Bad Bitch Benchmark first, they would have offered me a quarter of my price. I accomplished my goal, gained the necessary experience, and leveraged that into getting my next client, who saw the kinds of results I could deliver and happily matched my Bad Bitch Benchmark.

BAD BITCHES LEAN BACK

Sometimes, no matter how much you try, a moment comes when you just have to walk away. If you've done the hard work, confirmed your Bad Bitch Benchmark, countered the offer, but someone is still giving you excuses or lowballing you, it's time to start looking for new options.

One of my mentees, Bri, had been working at a firm for three years. She had started at the bottom as an intern and moved her way up from there; she was now at the VP level. But when she told me her salary, my mouth almost dropped to the floor. Given the years she had been at the startup and her value add, her salary was significantly below market value. The problem was, she had initially started as an intern, and so her internal benchmark was against her first salary and didn't account for the industry average. When she asked for a raise, her boss deflected and stated there was "no more budget." But as more and more people were getting hired and promoted around her, she started to wonder, *Is there really no budget or am I just undervalued at this company?* She was hitting all her targets, and her boss often complimented her for being a hard worker and good performer, so she knew it wasn't about the quality of her work. The last straw was when she discovered that a male junior associate who had just been hired three months ago was being paid nearly the same amount she was. She felt rightfully resentful and angry so I encouraged her to make a list of all her bottom-line contributions to the company so she would be ready to negotiate her raise. When she approached her boss, he continued to deflect, using the tired excuse of "That wouldn't be fair to other members of the team." Believe me, people will do everything in their power to deflect responsibility for paying you more if they can. I once asked a CEO directly for a raise, and he told me he didn't have the power to make that decision. Really? If the CEO can't influence that decision, who can?

Bri had hit a wall, so she needed to do something drastically different. She had been overextending herself trying to showcase she was worthy of a promotion, but that clearly was not working, and no matter how much more she did, she would continue to hit the same wall. Bri needed to lean back. When I tell a Bad Bitch to lean back I mean stop *leaning in* and trying harder and start *leaning back* and do just enough so they see how much value they are losing when they don't have your full effort. Because guess what? You've been taken advantage of if you have been giving 100 percent effort but only getting a fraction of what you're worth. That's a good girl mistake. If a Bad Bitch is going to give 100 percent effort, then they better pay you for 100 percent of your worth. Otherwise you start looking elsewhere.

So she did exactly that. Bri still showed up for the work, but she started leaning back and setting boundaries. She said, "No, I can't do this right now if it's not absolutely urgent." "No, I don't have the bandwidth unless I have an additional budget." This also gave her the time she needed to start considering other options. As she started leaning back, I advised her to start sending her résumé to other companies. A Bad Bitch always has options because options give you power. A few months later, her boss summoned her directly. When he asked her to cover his additional work, she stated that she was already at capacity and that the work was above her current pay grade. Not only did she make clear the value of her contributions, she also showed that she was irreplaceable. When he asked her what she needed, she leaned back and stated she was dissatisfied with her compensation. This time? He acquiesced, and the missing budget magically appeared.

If you're just starting out in your career, you may think you can't lean as far back as Bri did; the fact is, it's all about the mindset. No matter what stage of your journey you are at, so long as you know you are putting in the work and delivering results, you deserve to be compensated for it. Sometimes, people will pay you compliments to placate you. They'll tell you you're doing a great job or you're a great team player, but then conveniently forget come bonus season. Don't let it slip. Compliments don't pay the bills; cash does. Come with a clear bulleted list of your contributions and let them know you want more. At the end of the day, don't ever let yourself believe, *I need them more than they need me*, because all companies need Bad Bitches. If they don't see your worth, you take your business to the next company that will.

GET IT ON PAPER

In private or casual conversations, people will say anything to butter you up and make deals seem sweeter than they are. Sometimes these conversations happen casually on the phone, over drinks, or over dinner; whatever it is, if someone promises you something in any sort of informal verbal capacity, *get it on paper*.

I once asked for a raise and my boss promised me my end-of-the-year bonus would bump me into the next salary bracket. He quoted a number and told me I could rest assured that I had his word. When I left the conversation, I felt momentarily appeased, but I also felt uneasy. Would he remember what he told me six months from now, or would he develop temporary amnesia and gaslight me come bonus season? Long story short, I didn't stay at that job long enough to find out. I left for numerous reasons, but that moment was absolutely a clue, because when I came back and asked my boss to put it in writing? He deflected once again and told me to "take his word for it."

In the world of business, you can rely on someone's word, or you can rely on physical proof. Whether it's a fifteen-page legal document or you have to resort to a signed bar napkin to write down the terms of a handshake deal, get a signature on an actual piece of paper. Not only does it make someone more inclined to follow through with the deal, but if push comes to shove, guess which one holds up in court? I'll take someone's signature over their word any day.

A Bad Bitch who knows her worth and commands it is a rare and powerful breed. Commanding your worth is not a matter of being liked, it's a matter of knowing your value and being paid accordingly. As a Bad Bitch, you have full control over how worthy and deserving you believe yourself to be. Remind yourself, *I am valuable, my time is valuable, my services are valuable, so if you want a piece of this, then pay me my worth.*

There will always be some people who tell you they can't afford you, or that you're too expensive. That means you're doing something right. The people who can't afford you are self-selecting out, which simply means you are creating room for the ones that can.

Remember, time is your most valuable resource, and the more time you spend considering cheap deals that don't pay you, the less time you are giving to opportunities and people who will. No matter what happens, a Bad Bitch is able to unapologetically command her worth, because not only does she know she deserves the best, she knows she always has options.

COMMANDMENT 9

A BAD BITCH INVESTS HER ASSETS

INVITATION TO INVEST

Despite spending years as an entrepreneur and coaching thousands of women to become stronger, more confident entrepreneurs themselves, I still didn't fully believe that I could make an impact by investing in startups myself. I falsely believed becoming a startup investor—also called an angel investor or venture capitalist (VC)—was something I needed to be "properly" trained in. Not only that, but more than 95 percent of venture capitalists are male, 70 percent are white, and 40 percent attended either Harvard or Stanford Business School, so it was easy to fall into the trap of believing that because I didn't fit the average startup investor profile, I couldn't be one. So, I continued to grow my coaching practice, working with female entrepreneurs on pitching, branding, and preparing their business models so they could confidently go out to raise funds. It was deeply fulfilling work, and my clients were Bad Bitches across the board. But no matter how impressive or how well prepared the founders were, they were still at the mercy of men with money.

It was frustrating, to say the least. These were incredible women who'd poured themselves into their business presentations, perfecting every last slide and speaking point until they could pitch in their sleep, yet I watched as the venture capital boys' club continued to shut the doors in their faces. One day, after another coaching client came back to me venting about the ignorance of one of the VCs she had just pitched, I started to think, *If* they *aren't willing to invest, then why don't I?*

Easier said than done, of course. I assumed that in order to invest, I would need hundreds of thousands of dollars to start, and even though I had built up my bank account, it was still difficult to pull the trigger on a check with that many zeroes. Plus, there were simply too many amazing companies I wanted to invest in. How could I decide?

That all changed when one entrepreneur reached out to me and said she was accepting smaller individual investments—$5,000—for her startup: a consumer health company that aligned with my mission to empower women to take charge of their bodies. Moreover, I saw the huge market potential and the opportunity to make both an impact *and* a profit. Her invitation to invest was exactly what I needed to completely shift my perspective on startup investing. I realized I could start making a difference with small amounts of money, and to top it all off, I had the real-world experience, expertise, and passion to bring even more value as an investor in female-led companies.

Making my first startup investment was easier than I thought. Once I had made my decision, all I had to do was commit my dollar amount, sign a few simple investor documents, wire the money, and voilà!—I was officially an investor with equity in a fast-growing startup. After I invested, I saw the impact I could make by contributing my expertise on top of my capital; not only was the founder able to use my investment to test new marketing strategies, but I was also able to mentor her to successfully create content that helped launch her product into the market. The hands-on nature of my first startup investment was so rewarding that I knew I wanted to find more female-founded companies to invest in, so I did what I do best—I took action.

I launched the Bad Bitch Investor Bootcamp to rally a community of women investors to share investment knowledge and deals so we could all grow exponentially. I created the Bad Bitch Pitch event for female founders to pitch their companies and started putting small investments into the startups that I believed in most. It was the most exhilarating experience. I had been an entrepreneur for almost a decade, and suddenly I was sitting on the other side of the table as a startup investor with a growing portfolio of Bad Bitch businesses. The best part? As those female founders became more successful, the investors did, too. Not only was I investing my assets but I was also investing in the founders and the startups building the world I wanted to see—a world run by Bad Bitches.

A SEAT AT THE INVESTMENT TABLE

Investing is the most powerful generator of wealth, which is why the investment profession has traditionally attracted the most ambitious and money-motivated individuals. Professional money managers at private equity funds, hedge funds, and venture capital funds generate trillions of dollars each year by investing other people's money, making it grow, and taking a hefty slice of all the profits. It's no surprise, then, that investments are almost entirely controlled by a small group of wealthy white men.

The amount of financial power that the wealthiest male investors have is staggering. Of the total $103 trillion in the asset management industry, female and nonwhite fund managers control a measly 1.3 percent of that. In the $2 trillion venture capital industry, women make up less than 5 percent of partners, and women of color make up a mere 1.7 percent. Let the magnitude of that stat sink in. Women are 50 percent of the world's population and control almost *none* of the investment dollars. The result? As we continue to see only men at the head of investment tables, we are led to believe that women are inferior at investing.

It's not just at the institutional level, either. Social media is saturated with self-proclaimed investment "gurus" who claim to have the silver bullet to getting rich quick. With masculine-coded words like "Bull," "Bear," and "Spread," and aggressive messaging about "getting an edge," "beating the game," and "FOMO, FOMO, FOMO," it's no wonder women feel alienated and put off by investing.

The consequences are undeniable. Across the board, only 33 percent of women feel comfortable making investment decisions, and a paltry 9 percent of women think they make better investors than men. As a result of this lack of confidence, 65 percent of women keep most of their assets in cash and 41 percent have no plans to invest that cash. To date, only 26 percent of women invest in the stock market, despite 41 percent of these same women viewing the market positively. With exhaustive messaging that women are simply "more risk-averse," it's no wonder these numbers are changing at a snail's pace.

As we start internalizing these beliefs, it becomes easier to convince ourselves that we are simply not fit for investing. We don't ask for a seat at the investment table. We get stuck in analysis paralysis, unable to start investing until we have diligently researched every last detail and are 100 percent ready (which we will never be). Or we get overwhelmed and decide we are not "math and numbers" people and push investing down the road. For those who grew up low-income or poor, the idea of taking that kind of risk and losing our hard-earned money through a bad investment is terrifying, so we cling to the illusion of safety through saving.

Similarly, it's easy to convince ourselves that we simply "don't have enough money to invest." But when we flip that idea on its head, it becomes clear that it's not about what we don't have *yet*, it's what we lose out on *if we never start*. Every year, inflation depletes the value of the money in your savings account. In other words, if you let your savings sit idle, you are actively losing money, even if you never spend a dime. You may not feel the immediate effects of inaction, but the long-term effects will compound, and not to your benefit.

Moreover, not investing means relying on a system that isn't doing us any favors. Today, women carry two-thirds of the $1.5 trillion student loan debt in America, and our earnings continue to lag behind. With the systemic barriers and wage gap that women continue to face in the workplace, by the time we hit retirement age, women cumulatively earn on average $1,055,000 less than men. It's not surprising, then, that women are 80 percent more likely to face poverty in retirement.

It's time to face the harsh reality: we cannot rise up if we rely on a financial system rigged against us and naively hope for handouts. Good girls rely solely on salary, putting their money into retirement accounts, ignorantly waiting until they're seventy to reap rewards. This is not how a Bad Bitch operates. A Bad Bitch takes the necessary steps to get into the investing game.

BECOME A BAD BITCH INVESTOR

Even if you've never invested before in your life, you can start regardless of your age, income, or experience. Let go of any lingering beliefs that you are not ready to be an investor. In fact, let's put to rest all the typical excuses: *I don't make enough money, I don't have enough knowledge, I don't have enough time* . . . The fact is, anyone can learn to invest; what's more, successful investments are often a function of being in the right communities and getting access to the best deals more than anything else.

No matter what the "get rich quick" influencers say, investing is a long-term game, and women tend to be better long-term players because we don't react to market fluctuations the same way men do. Women trade 40 percent less frequently than men and change their portfolio asset allocation 20 percent less frequently. While men may make some short-term gains, overall impulsive extra trading has been shown to reduce their net returns by 2.65 percent a year, as opposed to a 1.72 percent increase for women. Even if women lack initial confidence in their ability to invest, we still tend to do it well. We may take more time to do our research, but when we make a decision, we commit, and we are in the investment for the long haul, to our benefit.

What does all this mean? It means that even if you are new to investing, as a woman, you have an inherent edge over the competition. If you are smart and capable of outperforming in other areas of your life, there is no reason to doubt that you will do the same when it comes to investing. Free yourself from the toxic belief that wealthy investors are a special breed of superhumans. They're not. They are normal people who figured out how to take a calculated and confident risk on investments they believed in.

To start investing, you don't need to know the ins and outs of business operations and financials; you don't need to understand all the jargon; you don't even need a lot of money. But you do need to become disciplined about your investment budget, do your own research, and get curious about industries and trends that will shape our future. Embrace the beauty of being a beginner, and always remember, there's no such thing as a stupid question.

That being said, Bad Bitches don't dwell on the basics and stay beginners forever. What's the difference between being a basic bitch investor and a Bad Bitch Investor? Easy. A basic bitch is content with simply learning the bare minimum and doing what everyone else does. They will simply put their money into retirement funds and passive index funds and not attempt to go any further. The basic bitch investor plays it safe. In most cases, they'll get a modest return on investment (ROI) when they retire.

A Bad Bitch Investor wants *more*. She's a leader who wants to build wealth *and* maximize the impact she can make with her dollar. As a Bad Bitch Investor, you make your money work for you *and* for the betterment of the world, and there is no better time than now to start.

WE CAN ALL BE STARTUP INVESTORS

While there are many asset classes you can invest in—from stocks (easily automated through ETFs), to crypto (new and volatile), to real estate (physical and location-dependent), as Bad Bitch Investors, we will focus on investing in startups, the asset class that has the greatest potential to maximize both profit *and* impact. Put another way, startup investing provides you with the potential opportunity to receive exponentially more ROI than traditional investments, while also being able to support the entrepreneurs and values you believe in.

When it comes to women becoming startup investors, we're talking about the potential to leverage our collaborative power like never before to create the world we want to see. When women invest, we are three times more likely to invest in female CEOs, so the more female startup investors, the higher the number of diverse and women-led businesses that get funded and succeed.

Now, you might be thinking, *Startup investing is only for rich bitches, and I don't have nearly enough money to invest yet*, but as I've mentioned before, this couldn't be further from the truth.

Traditionally, on top of being a male-dominated field, startup investing was reserved for the ultra wealthy. You had to be an *accredited investor*—in other words, you had to own at least $1 million in assets, or make an income of $200,000 per year in each of the previous two years, to invest in high-growth startup opportunities. Unsurprisingly, this created a dynamic where a homogenous group of primarily straight, white, cismale investors were the only ones that could access these types of investments. The profits flowed and the nouveau riche venture capital boys' club inevitably formed: Billy was funding Bob's startup, Bob was funding Tom's startup, Tom was funding Joe's startup, and before we knew it, a highly skewed and biased investment landscape formed where less than 2 percent of funding was going to female-founded startups and less than .35 percent to Black women. It's the white heteropatriarchy at its finest: the rich get richer, the walls get higher, and everyone else stays outside in the cold.

What changed? In 2015, the SEC established a new rule that demolished these exclusive barriers and made it so that anyone, regardless of income, could invest in startups if they chose. This meant exponentially more people could have a hand in funding the types of companies that would directly shape our collective future. For the first time, people of every color, sexuality, gender expression, and income level could consider startup investing as a viable option, and founders finally had the opportunity to seek funding from their communities and the world at large, no longer forced to rely on the old rich white boys' club.

While change hasn't happened overnight (the best things take time), we've already seen a significant shift in the numbers: female-founded crowdfunding campaigns are 32 percent more successful at reaching their funding target than those led by men. Why? Because they are using their collaborative superpowers to rally their communities around them. There is hope for the future as more diverse, immigrant, female-founded, and socially impactful businesses are finally receiving the money they deserve and rewarding new investors with significant payouts. But this is only the beginning. We've got a long way to go before we reach true equity, and it's going to be a hard fight to get there.

DIVERSIFY YOUR ASSETS

Now that we've discussed the social impact of startup investing, it's important to understand the financial impact of it. With startup investing, you have the potential to earn 1,000x or more on your initial investment because you are investing in a company at its earliest stages.

To put it into context, if you had invested $10K into Airbnb's earliest funding round, you could easily be retired, rolling in over $100 million in dough. That's a pretty sweet profit. Today you can find startup opportunities online in everything from tech to consumer goods to social justice and start investing with as little as $100. But how much money should you set aside for your startup investments? How many startups should you invest in?

Before we get into the nitty-gritty, keep in mind the golden rule of investing: *Diversify, diversify, diversify.* In other words, don't put all your eggs into one basket. As a Bad Bitch Investor, you want to think about startup investing in the context of your greater investment portfolio with a range of profiles, including lower-risk (e.g., index funds), medium-risk (e.g., real estate), and higher-risk (e.g., startups, art, crypto) to balance out risk and reward in your investments.

A good rule of thumb is to set aside 5–10 percent of your overall investment portfolio into high-growth startup investments. Of course, this isn't financial advice, and every individual situation is unique, so be honest with yourself about what your budget allows and your own risk tolerance, and go into any investment with the knowledge that *If I were to lose 50 or 100 percent of what I put in, it would not derail me.*

Within your startup investment budget, you also want to invest in a mix of industries and aim to diversify across at least twenty or more startup deals in your portfolio over time with the hope that at least a few will pay off in a big way. No matter how much you love a particular startup, never bet all your money on it. You don't ever want to be in a position where your sole investment fails and you're left with nothing.

Rather, take a disciplined diversification approach: take your startup investment budget and divide that by twenty to figure out how much you want to invest across startups over the next few years. For example, if you have $2,000, you want to invest $100 into twenty companies rather than $2,000 into the first one that catches your interest. If you have $20,000, the same logic applies: you want to invest $1,000 across twenty companies instead of your $20,000 all at once. Hypothetically, even if sixteen of your investments fail, one of them does super well, returning 50x, one of them does great at 10x, and two of them do pretty well at 5x, you'll end up with a 250 percent return.

All that said, none of this is guaranteed. No matter what investment you make, there is always a risk you could lose everything. Fearing loss is part of human nature, but as the saying goes, "Nothing ventured, nothing gained." That's why it's even more important to spread your investments across a portfolio of low-risk *and* high-reward investments.

Just remember, with almost all investments, you have limited risk—the greatest amount you can lose is the amount you put in. On the flip side, startup investing provides an unlimited upside—the potential for exponential gains if a startup eventually gets acquired or goes public.

Ask yourself, *What is the worst-case scenario for my investments? What is the best-case scenario?* Only invest what you are willing to lose, but be sure to balance that cautiousness with ambition; don't be afraid to dream about how much you could gain if you made even a few successful startup investments. With startup investing, you're accepting greater risk for a greater reward. That reward could mean the difference between retiring early and never retiring at all.

Remember how I said investing is a game? Well, the good news is, there's never been a better time to start playing. As any successful investor will tell you, the best time to start investing was twenty years ago, and the next best time to start is today.

YOUR BAD BITCH INVESTMENT PORTFOLIO

When I first launched the Bad Bitch Investor Bootcamp, women gave me all kinds of excuses as to why they were afraid to start investing: "I'm not good at finance. I don't know anything about venture capital. I don't know where to find startups. I don't understand the tech industry. I don't have the right network. I don't trust myself to make good investments . . ."

Across the board, these women vastly underestimated how much they already knew. But it quickly became clear that it wasn't that they weren't capable enough or smart enough to invest; they simply lacked the initial confidence to take that first step.

The truth is, you don't have to be an expert in startups, technology, or finance; you just have to know yourself and have confidence in your own observations of the world. Your startup investments should be in companies that align with your expertise, your values, and your vision of the future. So think of your Bad Bitch Portfolio—your unique collection of startup investments—as a reflection of these three pillars: what you *know*, what you *envision*, and what you *believe in*.

Invest in What You Know

Everyone is knowledgeable in their own way, and startup investing is about leveraging your areas of expertise into smart investments. As a consumer, you interact with a wide variety of companies every single day, and those companies spend millions of dollars to understand the views, opinions, and shopping habits of consumers just like you. As a startup investor, you can make educated guesses about the industries you know, the products you buy, and the brands you believe in.

What kinds of experiences have you had? What industries have you worked in? What types of businesses are you familiar with? What brands and products do you use the most? Understanding your own expertise and experience is the quickest path to finding your first great startup investment. For example, if you work at a real estate firm, consider exploring real estate tech startups to start. Not only can you leverage your industry knowledge, you'll also be able to more easily tap into other resources and contacts that are in your network to get a grasp of the types of innovation that are coming out of the sector. Or let's say you worked in the retail and fashion industry for years; since you already have a finger on the pulse when it comes to trends, you can more readily predict what will be successful in the future. You could ask yourself, *Where will the future of fashion be ten years from now? Will it be sustainable fabrics and dyes? Will it be more efficient supply chains?* By getting curious about the nature of the retail business and how it will change over the next decade, you'll be more aware of the types of innovations and startups you are most excited about in the industry.

Invest in What You Envision

Startup investing is a long-term game where you're making a bet on what will be successful in the future, factoring in changing economic systems, technological advancements, and human behavior. The best way to figure out what new industries to invest in is to envision how people will use technology in the future. You can have fun with it and ask big philosophical questions like: *What are the biggest problems that will impact humanity? What new technology will people need to solve those problems?*

You should also consider if the tech we use today will still be relevant ten years from now: *Will people still be using the iPhone ten years from now? Will streaming platforms still exist ten years from now? Will people still be driving cars ten years from now?*

It's incredible to think about how much technology and society have changed in just the last decade. Going forward, the pace of innovation will only get faster, so it's even more important to ask strategic and forward-thinking questions to have an edge on your investing journey.

The benefit of investing in a startup means that once you're invested in their journey, you'll get to learn alongside them. You'll be able to dive deeper into new technologies, observe trends as they develop, and apply that knowledge to other investments you make now and in the future.

Invest in the Future You Believe In

We live in a world where people are suffering from inefficient health care, economic insecurity, unchecked privacy breaches, and gross inequality. Across all industries, women are overlooked, undervalued, and underfunded. But for the first time, we have direct access to make a difference in solving these problems by investing in the causes we care about most and the leaders who share our vision for the world.

Going forward, the fastest-growing startups will be the ones that have a double bottom line of profit and positive impact, either on a community, a place, or a previously unmet or underserved need. The companies that will receive funding and be most likely to succeed are the ones that will intentionally uproot systemic issues, and in their place build more transparent, sustainable, and collaborative systems.

What problems do you care about solving? Food insecurity? Energy inefficiency? Discrimination and inequality? Startup investing is the only kind of investment where you get direct access to the founders' vision to change the world from the very beginning. Through investing, you have the influence to use your dollar to empower diverse founders and help build the future you believe in. Make your money work for the betterment of the world.

BAD BITCH INVESTOR BOOTCAMP

Before Sara joined the Bad Bitch Investor Bootcamp, she had just made her first startup investment . . . and immediately regretted it. Her mistake? She had invested in a company that the guys around her were hyping up to be a billion-dollar opportunity, and she'd felt pressured to invest quickly to get in on the deal. Unfortunately, shortly after the investment round closed, it became clear that the company barely had a functioning product, and the two male cofounders had lied about the progress of the company. Like many amateur investors, Sara had made the mistake of following the hype.

In startup investing, it's easy to get distracted by the newest, shiniest thing, especially as news headlines love to highlight investments that raise boatloads of money. But boatloads of money doesn't guarantee a good investment. There's no shortage of Silicon Valley tech startups that raised millions of dollars because they were great at creating FOMO among circles of investors, only to get exposed for lying or go bankrupt shortly thereafter.

Just because everyone is investing in certain companies when they think they're doing well doesn't mean you should, too. Don't make the mistake of getting caught up in the crowd.

Be wary of language like:

FOMO: "Everyone is investing. It's a once-in-a-lifetime deal."

Hyperbole: "This is a multibillion-dollar company in the making."

Urgency: "Our investment round is closing tomorrow. Are you in?"

Secrecy: "We can't share that information, we don't want people to steal our idea."

Scarcity: "We only have room for one more investor, so you need to let us know now."

In my experience, success doesn't come from following the pack—it comes from finding opportunities in places no one else is looking.

Even though Sara's first investment had left a sour taste in her mouth, she had responsibly diversified her investment budget beforehand and was determined to build her Bad Bitch Portfolio. Going forward, the most important thing for her would be to establish an investment process for properly evaluating startups so she wouldn't be fooled into making another investment she regretted. Through the Bad Bitch Investor Bootcamp, she learned the 6Ts framework for evaluating startup opportunities, which includes asking questions in six key areas:

1. **TEAM:** Is this the right team to execute on this business? Do they have the relevant track record or experience? Do the founders/team have aligned vision and complementary skill sets?

2. **TAM (TOTAL ADDRESSABLE MARKET):** How big is the market opportunity? Is there a clear customer persona that the business is targeting? How is the company planning to capture their target market (aka go-to-market strategy)?

3. **TECH:** How innovative is this technology? How does it compare to other similar technologies on the market? What is their competitive advantage?

4. **TRACTION:** Is there evidence that customers want or need this product? Does the company have realistic, achievable, and ambitious milestones? Is the business model scalable and able to withstand more customers over time?

5. **TIMING:** Why does this company need to exist *now*? Are there any social, economic, or technological forces that make this business more likely to succeed?

6. **TERMS:** Is the valuation of this company in line with the company's current stage of growth?

By using this framework, Sara could go into future investment deals with solid questions to ask the founders so she could form an educated opinion about whether or not the business was one she felt confident investing in.

When it comes to evaluating deals, you must ask yourself, *Have I done the proper due diligence to feel confident about making this investment?* and from there, check in with your gut as to whether this is truly a company you can feel good about supporting long term. (Go back to the three pillars—does this align with what you *know*, *envision*, and *believe in?*)

Armed with the 6Ts framework, you now have the foundation for evaluating your first startup investment. But how do you find high-quality investment opportunities? There are two options:

1. **INVEST ALONE:** If you are a beginner and dipping your toe in, there are numerous sites where you can now access startup deals; however, navigating these platforms alone can be overwhelming if you don't know what you're looking for—you can easily end up going down a rabbit hole. This is a big gamble and often a waste of time when faced with an ocean of opportunities that don't align with your values. The hardest and most time-consuming part of the startup investing process is not *investing itself*; it's finding great companies to invest in.

2. **INVEST IN A COMMUNITY OF BAD BITCHES:** Let's face it, investing is lonely; moreover, it's inefficient. As a Bad Bitch Investor, you don't have to invest alone. You want to minimize your time spent

finding and researching deals and maximize your access to high-quality investment opportunities. That's why I created the Bad Bitch Investor Bootcamp: to connect a community of Bad Bitches who are all committed to learning, investing, and growing together. We listen to Bad Bitch pitches, we put the 6Ts framework into practice, and we all bring investment deals to the table that align with our shared desire to uplift women-led businesses.

As any investor will tell you, the best way to learn is by doing, so the only way you will become a Bad Bitch Investor is by taking action and investing. Remember, wherever you are in your journey, you can have a seat at the investment table. Your dollar has a lot more power than you think, and even if you just have a tiny amount to invest, you can make a difference. For early-stage startups, the ability to raise money from Bad Bitch Investors like you gives the power back to the people instead of just the ultra wealthy. Taking charge of your assets and investing in a future that is inclusive and sustainable is one of the most empowering things you can do with your money. By becoming Bad Bitch Investors together, we can do more than any one of us alone can possibly imagine.

BAD BITCHES BUILD EMPIRES TOGETHER

OUR GREATEST SOURCE OF POWER

On a crisp autumn evening, I stood on my balcony looking out at the New York skyline, remembering how much hope and possibility I'd once seen in it. When I was just starting my career, the buzzing energy of the city motivated me to work harder, climb higher, and fight harder, but nearly a decade later, tired and worn down, I saw the towering buildings as symbols of my insignificance more than anything else.

After pouring years of my time, energy, and money into coaching, educating, and now investing in female entrepreneurs, I was confronted with the harsh truth: Not only had overall funding for women barely budged since I started, it had moved backward, reaching a five-year low, and it was clear that the very investors who claimed to "support" women were still using the same old playbook of excuses:

"I support women, but I can't invest because I don't have the budget anymore."

"I get the diversity angle, but I can't sacrifice returns."

"I don't think there are enough female founders to invest in."

I felt utterly defeated. No matter how much I tried, I felt like I was barely making a dent. I had started with an idealistic vision a decade ago, and now it was just that: an ideal, not a reality.

What's the point? I wondered. For the first time in my career, I contemplated giving it all up. Why fight an uphill battle when it would be so much easier to get a good job, earn a nice salary, accept the patriarchal status quo, and let someone else fight the hard fight?

It was in that state of powerlessness that I decided to try something drastically different. Before I quit for good, I needed to dig deep within myself to see if I had truly exhausted all my power. I needed to see my work and life from a fresh perspective; from experience, I knew the only way to do that was by pushing myself completely out of my comfort zone. As with any new endeavor, I researched all my options, from silent meditation to hot yoga to surfing retreats, until I finally landed on ayahuasca—the indigenous South American feminine plant medicine, known for its spiritual awakening powers. So, as a businesswoman who previously didn't have any spiritual inclinations, I swapped the concrete jungle for the real jungle and embarked on my first spiritual retreat with ayahuasca in Costa Rica. Now, surrounded by Mother Nature, I vocalized my intention to myself for my ayahuasca journey: "I want to meet my most powerful and authentic self." Repeating that intention, I drank the medicine, sat back, closed my eyes, and waited for the journey to begin.

◆ ◆

"Make it stop!" I screamed, tears streaming down my face. I clutched my stomach, my entire body shaking in pain unlike anything I had ever experienced before. It emanated from deep within me, overtaking me from the inside out until I finally surrendered, accepting that the pain was more powerful than me.

In the ensuing silence, I heard a humming sound. It started out slowly, growing gradually and building strength until it became a chorus of thousands of women. In the distance I saw a white cloud, and as I strained my eyes, the cloud came closer. That's when I saw her . . . and her . . . and her. I had never believed in spirits before, but there they were standing right in front of me, behind me, and beside me. One by one, they came up to me until I was completely surrounded.

"Who are you?" I whispered. They did not respond, but they didn't have to. I saw the pain in their eyes and the scars on their bodies, and it dawned on me, the pain I was experiencing was not mine alone. This was the cumulative pain of generations of women before me who had been abused, silenced, and defeated at the hands of a ruthless patriarchal world that never respected women as equals, as their own autonomous beings, and now they were visiting me to send me a message. *Keep going. Our power is already within you.*

I realized what true power was in that moment. It was not one woman fighting alone, sacrificing herself, and "doing it all" herself. True power was coming together as a collective and leveraging the greatest source of strength we all have—each other. Through that experience, I finally got the kick in the ass I needed to break free of any lingering traces of Good Girl Brainwashing—the people-pleasing, the self-doubt, the fear of failure—to embrace the full power that was not only already within me, but all around me.

On that journey in the jungle, I realized that the spirit and strength of generations of women who had fought and died for the freedoms we have today were living inside me. Inside all women. And it was on us to make sure that their work was not done in vain. Fighting for women's rightful place in the world is not just a nice thing to do, it is imperative. The mission is so much greater than all of us individually, and the only way we have a fighting chance to see true gender equality within our lifetimes is for us to join forces and harness our collective power together.

OVERTURN THE SYSTEM

We cannot assume that deeply embedded patriarchal systems will change just because we want them to. To go from surface-level awareness to generation-shifting change, it's not going to take the effort of one woman, it's going to take an empire of Bad Bitches who will come together and break barriers to radically transform the state of business and society as we know it. Across all major industries, especially the most powerful ones, there is significant room for improvement.

In big business, over 90 percent of Fortune 500 CEOs are white men, and there are more of them named Jo(h)n (5.3 percent) or David (4.5 percent) than there are women CEOs in total (4.1 percent). The result is a corporate structure in which outspoken women are silenced, pregnant women are punished, and women's workforce dropouts are on the rise, costing the US economy a whopping $650 billion annually.

Across the global healthcare system, women make up 70 percent of the global health workforce, but only 5 percent of healthcare leaders. The result is a preposterously biased and uneven system where women pay over 80 percent more in annual healthcare costs but receive inconsistent, low-quality service that often treats women's bodies not as our own, but as the property of men.

In the global financial system, women account for less than 2 percent of financial institutions' CEOs and less than 20 percent of executive board members. The result is that 42 percent of women worldwide—

about 1.1 billion—remain outside the formal financial system, without a bank account or basic tools to manage their money.

The list could go on, but you get the point: we are still stuck in nasty cycles that perpetuate male power and promotion from inner circles, leaving women largely excluded from leadership. The consequences of this are dire. When women are not represented in rooms in which important decisions are made, our bodies, our boundaries, and our bank accounts suffer.

However, there is hope. We are at one of the most critical inflection points in history: By the end of 2030, there will be the largest generational transfer of wealth into women's hands. Women in the US are expected to control $30 trillion, or two-thirds of the country's wealth. Globally, women are projected to control $97 trillion in wealth. If harnessed correctly, women can become the greatest economic force and change agent the world has ever seen. We are not just claiming equality; we are overturning an unfair system that's been in place for almost all of civilization. To do this means shifting our focus from individual change to collective action.

COLLABORATION OVER COMPETITION

This is the most urgent and important moment for Bad Bitches to rise together; to do so successfully, we must embrace the power of collaboration over competition. Think about it: How do men do business? Like a team sport. When they get together, they talk shop, they share deals, they combine resources, and most importantly, they invest in each other. Whether it's funding a buddy's company, sponsoring another man's promotion, or investing in another man's fund, men see investing as an opportunity to leverage their money for personal and mutual gain—in other words, to have their money make *more money*. Men love a good bet, and they know the odds of a successful business investment only improve when there are other guys in on the deal.

Women, on the other hand, have never been conditioned to see business as a team sport. For generations, women have had to rise alone. The old belief that there was only room for "one woman at the top" created a phenomenon called "queen bee syndrome," whereby the very women who fought tirelessly to break into the boys' club turned around and not only did not support younger women coming up the ladder behind them, but actively worked to push them down. The result is a catfight culture in which women are expected to work as individuals rather than a team, to doubt one another rather than invest in one another. Not only does this hurt our ability to rise individually and collectively, it benefits the men at the top; so long as we keep fighting among ourselves, we will never realize how powerful we can be together.

By the time I was actively startup investing, I knew the time had come to end this dynamic once and for all. The Bad Bitch Dream? A global collective of women who get unapologetically rich together and pour millions of dollars into female-led businesses that solve the greatest systemic challenges facing us now and in the future. By harnessing our collective power and investing in one another, we would no longer need to beg for a seat at the boys' table. We would create our own table to build unapologetic worth and wealth, and finally be able to invest in the diverse leaders that could impact the decisions that affect all of us, not just men.

When it came to naming this collective, I had a few options. Bad Bitch Network? Boring. Bad Bitch Ventures? Generic. I needed something that encompassed the magnitude of the vision. I wasn't just setting up an LLC, because this wasn't a company—this was an *empire*.

In the past, I would have worked on this vision in private, quietly relying on my hyperindependence to figure everything out myself, but this time I knew it was not only okay, it was imperative to rally support, so I started to spread the word publicly: I launched the *Bad Bitch Empire* podcast, began distributing a weekly newsletter, and hosted events across the US to galvanize women around the mission of investing and building unapologetic worth and wealth together.

Even when I was censored by LinkedIn and rejected for incorporation by the states of Delaware and New York for the use of the word "bitch," I kept speaking up and getting the word out. I knew that the right women would show up. After months of promotion and events, I started to attract the Bad Bitches that I had always wanted to be surrounded by—the unapologetic barrier breakers, the outspoken fighters, and the die-hard collaborators. These were the women who not only believed in the vision of collective change, but they also understood the power of collaborative investment.

First there was Nicole. She discovered the Bad Bitch Empire on Twitter, and the vision immediately resonated. At the time, she worked in medical device sales and had seen firsthand the challenges facing women's health leadership. She knew that if she wanted to create change, she needed to start investing in the types of healthcare companies she believed in—the ones that were built by and made for women.

Next there was Alexandra. Working in corporate finance by day, she was itching to make an impact through investing. She loved learning about new business ideas, and her Bad Bitch Dream was to become a full-time investor in female-led companies. She joined the Bad Bitch Empire to level up with a community of powerful women and jumpstart her investing knowledge.

Then there was Kaylan, an outspoken lawyer turned tech entrepreneur who was passionate about combining her passions for investing in women and crypto. Kaylan had spent her entire career fighting to be taken seriously in male-dominated rooms and couldn't wait to be surrounded by other Bad Bitches. She joined the empire to share her experience, skills, and capital to uplift the next generation of female leaders.

These women didn't seem to have much in common at first glance. They came from different backgrounds, different roles, different generations, and different industries. But there was one thing they all shared: even though they were already powerful on their own, they knew they could be far more powerful together.

What started as a vision, to build an empire of Bad Bitches with shared investments and shared success, soon became a reality. There are now women around the world who are collaborating to invest millions of dollars into female-led businesses, and now you can, too. No matter where you work or where you live, what field you're in, or how much money you make, you are invited to join the Bad Bitch Empire. When you do, rest assured: we're ready for you.

MORE BAD BITCHES, MORE MONEY

"When we invest together, we win together." This is one of the tenets of the Bad Bitch Empire, and it's because we know that investing in women isn't just the right thing to do, it's the smart thing to do. Too often, we hear the topic of investing in women categorized as impact or charity work. But it's time we changed this perception once and for all by arming ourselves with objective data:

Women Are the Most Powerful Economic Force

In the United States, women now control 85 percent of consumer spending and influence 70 percent of household financial decisions for themselves and for their families. Women are becoming more educated and ambitious than ever, outpacing men in higher education, earning 60 percent of undergraduate and graduate degrees, and entering the workforce at record rates. In 40 percent of US households, women are now the primary breadwinners. On a global level, the female economy is set to outpace some of the biggest nations' economies in the next five years. The economic force of women in the market cannot be underestimated, and it's not slowing down anytime soon.

Women Are Driving Innovation

Despite the growing economic force of women, the male-centered business world is still woefully behind. Consider the preexisting state of innovation: When airbags were first released, hundreds of women and children were injured or killed when the bags deployed. The reason? The group of male engineers who designed them didn't think to test their product on female crash test dummies. Similarly, when health trackers were first released, not a single Apple Watch or Fitbit considered a period tracker, despite that being the number one indicator women track. The reason? They didn't consult a female product manager. When AI algorithms were first introduced for recruitment, companies automatically rejected qualified female candidates. The reason? The existing algorithms written by men—with their own biased data sets and experiences—favored the standard heterosexual white male applicant, making it near impossible for those who didn't fit the mold to even have a chance at success.

By and large, men are still the default standard for product design. As a result, women, especially Black women and women of color, have had to suffer silently while paying an extra pink tax for years . . . but not anymore.

Going forward, "Just make it pink" will no longer be an acceptable solution for designing products for women. Unlike our predecessors, women today are increasingly unwilling to settle for products and services that do not align with our values or take our needs into account. The days of men building, designing, and selling products to women are over. As we continue to increase our purchasing power, the rise of women-centered innovation is undeniable. The next wave of billion-dollar businesses will be led by women that understand and address the needs of all women; investors who get ahead of the curve will be the ones who profit most.

Women Are the Largest Market Opportunity

Women are 51 percent of the population, control 85 percent of all consumer spending, yet receive only 2 percent of venture capital funding. Clearly there is a massive disconnect. At the Bad Bitch Empire, we see this disconnect as an incredible opportunity. We recognize the collective financial and social power women have in determining the types of companies that will succeed in the future. The fact that 90 percent of male-led investment firms are woefully unprepared to capitalize on the value of the women's market means that we have the opportunity to invest early in this next generation of female-led companies and influence change in the long term. The same female founders that have been overlooked, undervalued, and underfunded for far too long are the very ones who will now begin to rise to the top. In the future, there is no doubt that the most successful companies will be reflective of the diversity and needs of the millions of women who want better not only for themselves, but for the generations rising up behind them.

Women Are Generating Greater Financial Returns

No matter what the stats say about women receiving less investment, let's focus on what matters: the profits. Even though women-led companies receive less investment dollars on average, they outperform male-only leadership teams, delivering more than 2x revenue per dollar invested. Diversity of thought breeds better returns. Women also don't have the liberty of throwing away millions of dollars and YOLOing the way that many men do. The fact that raising money is harder for women means we must be more thoughtful and intentional with every dollar we spend. Intentionality is a virtue at the earliest stages of building companies, and it flows to the top. Comparing returns of Fortune 1000 companies led by female CEOs versus S&P 500, female-led companies saw an astounding 226 percent higher returns. The more we invest in Bad Bitches, the more money we all stand to make.

Now when I have conversations with ignorant or skeptical investors who use those tired old lines, I am armed with data to back up my responses:

- When they say: "Women are not a big enough market opportunity,"
  I say: "Women control 85 percent of consumer spending, influence 70 percent of household decisions, and are on track to outpace some of the biggest nations' economies in the next five years. Do you really want to bet against us?"

- When they say: "It's cute to invest in women's businesses,"
  I say: "Women represent the largest market opportunity in history, underserved and undervalued. The fact that 90 percent of male-led investment firms have not yet caught on is a massive opportunity for us."

- When they say: "I can't sacrifice returns,"
  I say: "Female leadership teams outperform male-only leadership teams, delivering more than 2x revenue per dollar invested, so investors who aren't actively pursuing investments in women founders are simply leaving money on the table."

The data is indisputable: the most powerful thing *anyone* can do is invest in women.

BAD BITCH EMPIRE STATE OF MIND

Having sat on both sides of the table as a serial entrepreneur and as a startup investor, I can confidently say that there is no greater feeling than having a vision of the world, especially one that doesn't yet exist, and turning it into reality. Especially when the odds are stacked against you. Not only is it incredibly satisfying to prove the haters and naysayers wrong, so is proving to *yourself* that you have it within you to succeed against all odds. Today, women are building businesses at faster rates than at any other point in our country's history, with women of color accounting for 89 percent of new businesses.

Of course, as incredible as this progress is, there is still significant room to grow. Less than 2 percent of women-owned businesses have hit the million-dollar annual revenue mark, so there is ample opportunity to build bigger, to build not only a business, but a Bad Bitch Business: one that recognizes the billion-dollar opportunity of unapologetically putting women's needs and perspectives first.

Every woman, by virtue of simply being and experiencing the world as she is, is now a walking treasure chest of billion-dollar Bad Bitch Business ideas that have never once occurred to a single CEO named John or David. If you have ever had an idea or even an *inkling* to start a business, especially one that solves a problem for other women, this is your sign to do something about it. Because if it's a pain point for you, it's a pain point for millions of women, and the beginning of an empire-building business idea.

For example, Julia, one of the women who pitched the Bad Bitch Empire in its early days, was building a business tackling menopause, a $600 billion market that had been uniformly ignored by male investors who did not believe this to be a "real market." Julia herself had experienced firsthand the lack of information, treatment, and support for women going through this process. Further in her research, she had discovered that 80 percent of women suffer life-disruptive menopause symptoms and over 70 percent were not addressed, resulting in everything from lower quality of life to higher healthcare costs to over $150 billion in lost work productivity. By cultivating a Bad Bitch Empire state of mind, Julia identified an untapped multibillion-dollar market that was highly lucrative if served correctly.

Now it's your turn.

If you want to start building your Bad Bitch Business, there are three primary questions I want you to answer for yourself, and for your future investors: *Why this problem? Why you? Why now?*

Why This Problem?

If you're ready to take the leap into entrepreneurship but not exactly sure what business idea to pursue, ask yourself: *What problem do I care most about solving?*

Start by thinking about a pain point you have personally experienced that could be a similar pain point for other women. For example, you might think about a daily experience as simple as going for a walk and remember the times you felt unsafe walking home at night. You're not alone. Eighty percent of women feel uncomfortable walking alone at night, and for good reason. Sixty-six percent of women aged sixteen to thirty-four have experienced one form of harassment in the previous twelve months, and 29 percent have felt like they were being followed. Given that being followed, harassed, and assaulted are almost universally shared experiences of being a woman, you might wonder, why aren't there more companies actively trying to solve this massive problem?

From here, you would start researching the competitive landscape. What preexisting companies are already tackling women's safety? What do they do successfully? What could they do better? What kind of technology are they using to solve the problem? Are there areas, regions, or subcategories of women's safety you are particularly interested in?

If you were interested in the subcategory of women's online safety, you would discover that women—especially women of color—are inordinately affected by cyberattacks and online harassment, while also being at an increased risk of financial data loss, violations of privacy, and security breaches. Moreover, there's a massive industry problem: women account for only two out of ten cybersecurity professionals, meaning there is an urgent need to create a cyberspace that is safer, more secure, and more inclusive. How big is the cybersecurity market? A whopping $10.5 trillion, and that number is only getting bigger. You have now identified a big problem, a big market, and the beginning of a Bad Bitch Business idea.

Whatever industry you want to tackle—from healthcare to travel to sustainable tech—this is your chance to think BIGGER and cultivate a Bad Bitch Empire state of mind. Don't preclude yourself by worrying about the logistics of solving the problem. For now, focus on getting a solid grasp of the problem and the market, then make sure the problem you choose is one you are passionate about solving so you will be motivated to continue building your business for years to come.

Why You?

Ask any investor, and they'll tell you that one of the most (if not *the* most) important factors in a new business is the founder or founding team. If you're serious about being an entrepreneur, investors will want to see that you have what it takes to turn your Bad Bitch Business idea into a billion-dollar empire. So, as you are deciding on your big problem, you also want to give thought to what your superpowers are, and how they might apply to your chosen business idea. Do you have a unique background or skill set that makes you particularly suited to building this business? Do you have industry expertise? Do you have extensive firsthand experience with this market that gives you unique insights on how to solve the problem?

When I started the Bad Bitch Empire I asked myself these questions as well. *Why am I the one to build this company? What unique skills, experiences, or insights do I have into the market of women's business, entrepreneurship, and investing?* First, I gained invaluable skills from launching, scaling, and selling my company, so I knew exactly how to support female business owners. Second, I had tackled my money mindset, built my investment portfolio, and was passionate about guiding women to invest and create even greater impact with their money. Finally, my extensive experience coaching women across industries gave me the unique ability to help women break free of Good Girl Brainwashing and unapologetically embrace their power. My experience and my passion, combined with my superpowers in branding, marketing, and community building, made me the best woman to build the Bad Bitch Empire.

Once you've answered the question "Why you?" don't fall into the trap of making this a one-woman show. As you build your business, enroll your community of Bad Bitches into your cause. Bounce business ideas off your friends, invite them to your events, ask them to spread the word, involve them in user research (ask survey questions like: Would they use your product or service? How does the messaging resonate with them? How much would they pay for it? Is it solving a real problem they have? What other features do they need?), and celebrate with them as your business grows.

Why Now?

You might have the right idea, the right expertise, and the right support, but sometimes the success of building a business can come down to luck and timing. Of course, you can never undervalue hard work, execution, a great team, or sufficient funding, but there are also countless instances when businesses bombed simply due to bad timing. For example, when the Covid-19 pandemic hit in early 2020, thousands of companies went out of business, not because they weren't good businesses, but simply because they were not prepared for a global pandemic that would fundamentally alter life as we knew it. While you can't control or 100 percent accurately predict the future, you can make a case for why *now* is the best time to build your Bad Bitch Business.

Ask yourself: *What makes the timing right for this company to succeed now? What are the social, economic, or technological forces that make this the moment to build your business? Is there an urgency to solve this problem? If so, why? What are the consequences of not solving this problem and building this business now?*

In Julia's pitch, for example, she made this case for why now is the best time to tackle the multibillion-dollar menopause market:

- **TECHNOLOGICAL FORCES:** Healthcare technology is rapidly evolving, and older women are being left behind. Not only is there a lack of transparency and data around menopause symptoms, healthcare services for women both online and offline are light-years behind where it should be.
- **SOCIAL FORCES:** The rising populations of Millennial and Gen-Z women have grown up with digital healthcare support for everything from periods to pregnancy. By the time they hit menopause, they will expect the same level of transparency and care.
- **ECONOMIC FORCES:** Combine the social rise of women with our rapidly increasing economic power and it becomes clear: by not preemptively building for this market now, we are leaving billions of dollars on the table.

By bringing these three forces together, Julia made a compelling case that menopause is not just a problem to solve eventually, it is one that needs to be tackled *now*. This is the level of preparation, urgency, and commitment that makes a business pitch impossible to ignore.

◆ ◆

When more women build, more women grow. When more women invest, more women rise. It is only by coming together that we will create a world where our bodies, boundaries, and bank accounts are given the respect they deserve.

You now have the awareness, the perspective, and the tools to break free of Good Girl Brainwashing once and for all. You do not need permission to be powerful. You are already powerful. So let this be your sign: *now* is the time to launch your Bad Bitch Dream, *now* is the time to invest in a Bad Bitch Business, *now* is the time to claim your space in the Bad Bitch Empire. Step up and help create the world you want to see. Even if you don't have it all figured out, just start, act, trust the process, and in doing so you will become the Bad Bitch you were born to be. Whether you're building, investing, or supporting, choose your path and commit to it wholeheartedly. You'll have an empire of Bad Bitches behind you the whole way through.

AUTHOR'S NOTE

BEHIND THE SCENES OF
THE BAD BITCH BUSINESS BIBLE

There's only one word that can properly encapsulate my author's journey writing *The Bad Bitch Business Bible* . . .

Excruciating.

I've built companies from scratch, I've raised millions of dollars in funds, I've competed at the highest athletic level, yet birthing this book was one of the most difficult, lonely, and painful experiences I've ever had.

There's something deeply intimidating about writing a book called *The Bad Bitch Business Bible*. Even though I came up with the original Bad Bitch concept that landed my dream book deal, it quickly became clear to me that I was still far from being the Bad Bitch I needed to be.

When I started writing, I thought the book would take me six months from start to finish, *easy*. But of course, I had no idea what was in store over the next two years.

First, the massive imposter syndrome. *Who am I to write this book? What if people think my writing sucks? What if no one buys the book?* Funny how the old good girl voices sneak back up on you.

Next, the self-induced pressure: *If I write this book, it has to be perfect. This book must be successful.*

Then, when I thought I had it all figured out, the book shined a glaring spotlight on all the ways I was *still* not a Bad Bitch. I started noticing times in my life when I was undervaluing myself, settling in my boundaries, and accepting bullshit from bros, and I realized I could not, in good faith, write *The Bad Bitch Business Bible* until I started practicing what I preached, until I truly embodied being a Bad Bitch in every aspect of my life.

Writing this book forced me to level up in ways I never imagined. It made me relive a lifetime of old good girl memories and trauma, while keeping me accountable to walking the Bad Bitch walk. Simultaneously, I was also going through significant changes in my career. I joined and left a full-time role at a tech company, I dove into advising crypto companies as the markets spiked and crashed, and I officially launched the Bad Bitch Empire into the world. What I didn't realize was that the hard lessons from this period in my life would be the exact ones I needed to learn in order to complete this book.

The woman I was when I started writing *The Bad Bitch Business Bible* is completely different from the one who finished it. In the beginning, my Bad Bitch self was an alter ego I secretly embraced, the words "Bad Bitch" softly mumbled under my breath. Today, I'm unapologetically living and breathing my Bad Bitch Energy.

I am clear on my purpose.

I am building our empire.

I am proud of the woman I'm becoming, every single day.

This book gave me the audacity to call myself a Bad Bitch, and I hope it does the same for you.

I can't wait to see you unleash your inner Bad Bitch into the world.

ACKNOWLEDGMENTS

First and foremost, thank you to my parents who gave me the foundation of unconditional love and support so I could unapologetically pursue my Bad Bitch Dreams. Thank you to my dad for being my inspiration and showing me the values of hard work and perseverance. You taught me to have high standards for myself and gave me the backbone of strength to face all of life's challenges with courage and grace. Thank you to my mom for being the kindest and most loving person in my life and for showing me that softness is also strength. Throughout the many challenges and breakdowns I had along the way in writing this book, you both made sure I never lost sight of my North Star: my purpose.

Thank you to my little brother, Jordan, for always keeping it real with me and being there for me in my moments of need.

My deepest gratitude to all my coaching clients, founders, students, and mentees who have worked with me over the years. You all inspire me and I'm so proud of how much you've accomplished. I would not be here without each and every one of you.

I'm especially grateful to the early Bad Bitch Empire team members, investors, and advisors who saw the Bad Bitch vision and supported me even in my moments of doubt. Thank you to Nicole Montoya, Kaylan Sliney, Alexandra Harris, Mitch Mechigian, Juliana Uto, Nadine Cino, Anna Roubos, and Lauren Shroll for anchoring me and helping me push forward.

To my agent, Jordan Hill, thank you for supporting me, advocating for me, and helping me stay grounded throughout the publishing process. Thank you to Joanna Volpe, Tracy Williams and the New Leaf Literary team for your support.

To the team at HarperCollins, thank you to everyone who made this book a reality. To my publisher, Hollis Heimbouch for believing in my vision from the very beginning and championing *The Bad Bitch Business Bible* throughout the entire process. To my editors, Wendy Wong for igniting the initial spark and Rachel Kambury for carrying the torch across the finish line. To Karintha Parker and Jessica Gilo and the entire marketing team for amplifying the book to new audiences. To those who helped make the book beautiful inside and out, Robin Bilardello, Janet Rosenberg, Nikki Baldauf, and Bonni Leon-Berman.

Thank you to Stephanie Kim who worked with me on the initial proposal and helped me secure the bag with my first book deal. Thank you to Steve Cohen for your initial introduction that kicked things off.

Thank you to Hilary Swanson who coached me throughout the writing process and helped me hone my no-nonsense Bad Bitch voice as an author.

Thank you to Alexa Gabriel for designing the first BBE dress and Sivan Miller for capturing a powerful image for the book cover.

To all the unapologetic, barrier-breaking Bad Bitches past and present who paved the way for women of our generation to be able to have the freedom and opportunities that we have today. Thank you for stepping into your power and refusing to settle. I am honored to have the opportunity to contribute to this divine mission of advancing women's rights and to play even a small role in the greater movement for gender equality.

And finally, to you, dear reader. Thank you for reading, sharing, and amplifying the message of this book. I am eternally grateful for your support.

NOTES

Introduction

xiv   60 percent of all undergraduate and graduate degrees: "Overview: Spring 2 022 Enrollment Estimates," National Student Clearinghouse Research Center, Spring 2022, https://nscresearchcenter.org/wp-content/uploads/CTEE_Report _Spring_2022.pdf.

xiv   five times the national average: "State of Women-Owned Businesses Report," National Association of Women Business Owners, 2016.

xiv   47 percent of the workforce: "The gender gap in employment: What's holding women back?" International Labor Organization, November 2021.

xiv $31 trillion in annual spending: "Globally, Women Performed an Estimated US$31.8 Trillion in Consumer Spending in 2019," Catalyst.org, 2019, https://www.catalyst.org/research/buying-power/.

xv   "suffering from natural defectiveness": Simone de Beauvoir, *The Second Sex* (London: Vintage Classics, 2015).

xx   Men occupy over 90 percent of Fortune 500 CEO roles: "Fortune 500 CEOs, 2000–2020: Still Male, Still White," The Society Pages, October 28, 2020, https://thesocietypages.org/specials/fortune-500-ceos-2000-2020-still-male -still-white/.

xx   75 percent of senior roles: Tomas Chamorro-Premuzic, "The Business Case for Women in Leadership, *Forbes*, March 2, 2022, https://www.forbes.com /sites/tomaspremuzic/2022/03/02/the-business-case-for-women-in-leader ship/?sh=3f55a5d39cbb.

xxiii $97 trillion by 2024: Anna Zakrzewski, "Managing the Next Decade of Women's Wealth," Boston Consulting Group, April 9, 2020, https://www.bcg.com /publications/2020/managing-next-decade-women-wealth.

xxiii   that's an additional $30 trillion: Pooneh Bag, "Women as the next wave of growth in US wealth management," McKinsey & Company, July 29, 2020, https://www.mckinsey.com/industries/financial-services/our-insights/wo men-as-the-next-wave-of-growth-in-us-wealth-management.

Commandment 1: A Bad Bitch Is Unbreakable

19   not pursuing their dream career: "Changing lanes: Are Americans in their dream career?" Moneypenny, 2021, https://www.moneypenny.com/us/re sources/blog/changing-lanes-are-americans-in-their-dream-career/.

Commandment 2: A Bad Bitch Takes Up Space

26   only 2 percent of funding: Q1 2022 PitchBook NVCA Venture Monitor, Pitch-Book, April 13, 2022, https://pitchbook.com/news/reports/q1-2022-pitch book-nvca-venture-monitor.

28   91 percent of women are unhappy with their bodies: Mario Palmer, "5 Facts About Body Image," *Amplify*, May 21, 2013, http://amplifyyourvoice.org/u /marioapalmer/2013/05/21/byob-be-your-own-beautiful.

28   Fifty-eight percent of college-age girls feel pressured: "Eating Disorders Statistics," *National Association of Anorexia Nervosa and Associated Disorders*, 2014, http://www.anad.org/get-information/about-eating-disorders/eating-dis orders-statistics/.

28   woman spends an average of seventeen years: "Women spend 17 years of their lives on diets," Diet Chef Study, *Marie Claire UK*, September 18, 2012.

Commandment 3: A Bad Bitch Asserts Her Voice

47   men speak 75 percent of the time: Christopher F. Karpowitz, "Gender Inequality in Deliberative Participation," *American Political Science Review*, August 2012.

47   interrupt women 33 percent more often: Adrienne Hancock, "Influence of Communication Partner's Gender on Language," *Journal of Language and Social Psychology*, December 2014.

48   45 percent of women say it's also difficult to speak up in virtual meetings: "Catalyst Workplace Survey Reveals Optimism About Gender Equity During Covid-19, but Skepticism on Commitment of Companies," Catalyst, June 30, 2020, https://www.catalyst.org/media-release/workplace-gender-equity-covid-19.

48   Jo(h)n or David than all women combined: Susanne Althoff, "Men named Jo(h)n have written as many of 2020's top business books as all women combined," *Fortune*, December 20, 2022, https://fortune.com/2020/12/20/women -bestselling-business-books-2020/.

48   80 percent of business school cases: Colleen M. Sharen, "Invisible or Clichéd: How Are Women Represented in Business Cases?" *Journal of Management Education* (November 9, 2018), https://doi.org/10.1177/1052562918812154.

49   America's Most Innovative Leaders, featuring 102 founders and CEOs, only one was a woman: "America's Most Innovative Leaders, *Forbes*, September 2019, https://www.forbes.com/lists/innovative-leaders/#79cfab8726aa.

Commandment 4: A Bad Bitch Owns Her Wins

67   84 percent of women feel uncomfortable promoting themselves: Mighty Forces, Southpaw Insights, Upstream Analysis, and Grey Horse Communi-

cation, "A Survey Exploring Women's Fear of Self-Promotion," The Self-Promotion Gap, November 2019, https://www.selfpromotiongap.com.

67   would prefer to run errands in the rain: Ibid.

67   strengths and weaknesses of the women at their firm: Priya Fielding-Singh, Devon Magliozzi, and Swethaa Ballakrishnen, "Why Women Stay Out of the Spotlight at Work," *Harvard Business Review*, August 28, 2018, https://hbr.org/2018/08/why-women-stay-out-of-the-spotlight-at-work.

69   bad team players and were even considered a threat: Liat Clark, "Study: women undervalue themselves when working with men," *Wired*, August 8, 2013, https://www.wired.co.uk/article/women-teamwork-bias.

69   admired for their ambition: Wilhelmina Wosinska, Amy J. Dabul, Robin Whetstone-Dion, Robert B. Cialdini, "Self-Presentational Responses to Success in the Organization: The Costs and Benefits of Modesty," *Basic and Applied Social Psychology* 18, no. 2 (1996): 229–42, http://doi.org/10.1207/s15324834basp1802_8.

69   take less credit for themselves: Michelle C. Haynes, "It Had to Be You (Not Me)!: Women's Attributional Rationalization of Their Contribution to Successful Joint Work Outcomes," *Personality and Social Psychology Bulletin*, May 7, 2013, https://journals.sagepub.com/doi/abs/10.1177/0146167213486358?journalCode=pspc.

79   inspired when they hear about other women's accomplishments: Mighty Forces, Southpaw Insights, Upstream Analysis, and Grey Horse Communication, "A Survey Exploring Women's Fear of Self-Promotion," The Self-Promotion Gap, https://www.selfpromotiongap.com.

Commandment 5: A Bad Bitch Curates Her Crew

86   95 percent of your success or failure in life: "[the people you habitually associate with] determine as much as 95 percent of your success or failure in life," David McClelland, Harvard University.

Commandment 6: A Bad Bitch Calls Out Bullshit

104   "Reflecting on One Very, Very Strange Year at Uber": Susan J. Fowler, "Reflecting on One Very, Very Strange Year at Uber," February 19, 2017, https://www.susanjfowler.com/blog/2017/2/19/reflecting-on-one-very-strange-year-at-uber.

104   across the tech and financial industries: "How a 26-year-old woman became the nemesis of Uber's work culture," *Economic Times*, October 26, 2017, https://economictimes.indiatimes.com/news/international/how-a-26-year-old-woman-became-the-nemesis-of-ubers-work-culture/reflecting-on-one-very-very-strange-year-at-uber/slideshow/61182575.cms.

104   over nineteen million times on Twitter: Haley Britzky, "#MeToo hashtag used over 19 million times on Twitter," *Axios*, October 13, 2018, https://www.axios.com/2018/10/13/metoo-hashtag-used-over-19-million-times-on-twitter.

104 69 percent of women have been sexually harassed: Nikki Graf, "Sexual Harassment at Work in the Era of #MeToo," Pew Research Center, April 4, 2018.

104 LGBTQIA+ workers also report experiencing sexual harassment: "Sexual harassment of LGBT people in the workplace," TUC, May 17, 2019, https://www.tuc.org.uk/research-analysis/reports/sexual-harassment-lgbt-people-workplace.

105 51 percent of women are physically touched without permission: "The Facts Behind the #MeToo Movement: A National Study on Sexual Harassment and Assault," *Stop Street Harassment*, January 2018, http://www.stopstreet harassment.org/wp-content/uploads/2018/01/Survey-Questions-2018-National-Study-on-Sexual-Harassment-and-Assault.pdf.

105 85 percent of victims never file a complaint with HR: Chai R. Feldblum & Victoria A. Lipnic, "Select Task Force on the Study of Harassment in the Workplace," U.S. Equal Employment Opportunity Commission, June 2016, https://www.eeoc.gov/select-task-force-study-harassment-workplace.

105 1 percent of victims ever confront their perpetrators: "26 Shocking Sexual Harassment in the Workplace Statistics," What to Become, September 13, 2022, https://whattobecome.com/blog/sexual-harassment-in-the-workplace-statistics/#stat11.

106 sexual harassment . . . costing $2.6 billion in lost productivity: "Report for the Sexual Harassment National Inquiry: The economic costs of sexual harassment in the workplace," Deloitte Access Economics, March 2020, https://www2.deloitte.com/au/en/pages/economics/articles/economic-costs-sexual-harassment-workplace.html.

Commandment 7: A Bad Bitch Loves Money

127 90 percent of money articles targeted toward women: Professor Shireen Kanji, "Summary Report: Gendered representations of money in visual media, a study," Starling Bank, May 2021, https://www.starlingbank.com/docs/reports-research/StarlingGenderRepresentationReport.pdf.

136 56 percent of married women leave investment . . . to their husbands: "Own your worth: How women can break the cycle of abdication and take control of their wealth," UBS Wealth Management USA, April 13, 2018, https://www.ubs.com/global/de/media/display-page-ndp/en-20180514-ubs-reveals-top-reason.html.

136 70 percent of women fire their male advisors within a year of their spouse's death: "The Future of Wealth is Female," Transamerica, January 2021, https://www.irionline.org/wp-content/uploads/legacy/default-document-library/272669_0121_women-and-investing-white-paper_final_021021-update_digital.pdf.

139 $5 million in fifty years at a 7 percent annual interest rate: Compound Interest Calculator, Investor.gov, US Securities and Exchange Commission,

https://www.investor.gov/financial-tools-calculators/calculators/compound
-interest-calculator.

Commandment 8: A Bad Bitch Commands Her Worth

144   majority of the college-educated workforce: Richard Fry, "Women now outnum-
ber men in the U.S. college-educated labor force," Pew Research Center, September 26, 2022, https://www.pewresearch.org/fact-tank/2022/09/26/women
-now-outnumber-men-in-the-u-s-college-educated-labor-force/.

144   Latina women comprising the biggest increase: Analilia Mejia, "Celebrating the Rise of Hispanic Women Workers," U.S. Department of Labor Blog,
September 17, 2021, https://blog.dol.gov/2021/09/17/celebrating-the-rise-of
-hispanic-women-workers.

144   twenty-four of the Fortune 500 companies are led by women: Emma Hinchl-
iffe, "Female CEOs run just 4.8% of the world's largest businesses on the
Global 500," *Fortune*, August 3, 2022, https://fortune.com/2022/08/03/female
-ceos-global-500-thyssenkrupp-martina-merz-cvs-karen-lynch/.

145   biggest drop-off point for women is the VP level: Tiffany Burns, Jess Huang,
Alexis Krivkovich, Ishanaa Rambachan, Tijana Trkulja, Lareina Yee, "Women
in the Workplace 2021," McKinsey & Company, September 27, 2021, https://
www.mckinsey.com/featured-insights/diversity-and-inclusion/women-in
-the-workplace.

145   60 percent of women never negotiate their first salary: "2020 U.S. compensation insights survey," Randstad USA, 2020.

146    $35,000 less in business financing than men: Jared Hecht, "State of Small
Business Lending: Spotlight on Women Entrepreneurs," Fundera by Nerd-
Wallet, February 2, 2021, https://www.fundera.com/blog/the-state-of-on
line-small-business-lending-q2-2016.

146   66 percent of the questions directed toward female entrepreneurs: Dana
Kanze, Laura Huang, Mark A. Conley, and E. Tory Higgins, "Male and Female Entrepreneurs Get Asked Different Questions by VCs—and It Affects
How Much Funding They Get," *Harvard Business Review*, June 27, 2017,
https://hbr.org/2017/06/male-and-female-entrepreneurs-get-asked-different
-questions-by-vcs-and-it-affects-how-much-funding-they-get.

Commandment 9: A Bad Bitch Invests Her Assets

161   Harvard or Stanford Business School: Simone Stolzoff, "Venture capital's diversity problem in two words: alma mater," *Quartz*, July 31, 2018, https://
qz.com/1343912/venture-capitals-diversity-problem-in-two-words-alma-
mater.

163    $103 trillion in the asset management industry: Lubasha Heredia et al., "The
$100 Trillion Machine," *Boston Consulting Group*, July 8, 2021, https://www.
bcg.com/publications/2021/global-asset-management-industry-report.

163   female and nonwhite fund managers control a measly 1.3 percent of that: "New

study shows diverse-owned firms represent a small fraction of asset management industry despite equal performance," Knight Foundation, January, 28, 2019, https://knightfoundation.org/press/releases/new-study-shows-diverse-owned-firms-represent-a-small-fraction-of-asset-management-industry-despite-equal-performance/.

163    $2 trillion venture capital industry: Rob Kozlowski, "Venture capital passes $2 trillion in AUM," *Pensions & Investments*, May 12, 2022, https://www.pionline.com/alternatives/venture-capital-passes-2-trillion-aum-preqin.

163   women of color make up a measly 1.7 percent: Women in VC, Report: The Untapped Potential of Women-Led Funds, October 2020, https://assets.ctfassets.net/jh572x5wd4r0/7qRourAWPj0U9R7MN5nWgy/711a6d8344bcd4fbe0f1a6dcf766a3c0/WVC_Report_-_The_Untapped_Potential_of_Women-Led_Funds.pdf.

164   9 percent of women think they make better investors than men: "2021 Women and Investing Study," Fidelity Investments, 2021, https://www.fidelity.com/bin-public/060_www_fidelity_com/documents/about-fidelity/FidelityInvestmentsWomen&InvestingStudy2021.pdf.

164   65 percent of women keep most of their assets in cash: "Women and Wealth: Fact Sheet," U.S. Trust Bank of America, 2013, http://girlsschools.org/wp-content/uploads/2017/11/Insights-on-Wealth-and-Worth-Women-and-Wealth.pdf.

164   26 percent of women invest in the stock market: Martina Chung et al., "The (Financial) Future Is Female," S&P Global, 2019, https://www.spglobal.com/_division_assets/images/womens-paper/241755-global_womens_investor_survey_paper_8.5x11_digital_final.pdf.

164   despite 41 percent of these same women viewing the market positively: Jodie Gunzberg, "Women are More Wary of Markets," S&P Global, 2019, https://www.spglobal.com/en/research-insights/featured/special-editorial/the-financial-future-is-female.

165   two-thirds of the $1.5 trillion student loan debt in America: "Deeper in Debt: Women and Student Loans," AAUW, 2021, https://www.aauw.org/app/uploads/2020/03/DeeperinDebt-nsa.pdf.

165   earn on average $1,055,000 less than men: "Women and Financial Wellness: Beyond the Bottom Line," Merrill Lynch, April 19, 2018, https://www.businesswire.com/news/home/20180419005028/en/Women-Have-Fundamentally-Different-Journeys-to-Financial-Wellness-Merrill-Lynch-Study-Reveals.

165   women are 80 percent more likely than men to face poverty in retirement: "Women 80% More Likely to Be Impoverished in Retirement," National Institute on Retirement Security, March 1, 2016, https://www.nirsonline.org/2016/03/women-80-more-likely-to-be-impoverished-in-retirement/.

166   Women trade 40 percent less frequently: "How America Saves 2021," Van-

guard, 2021, https://institutional.vanguard.com/content/dam/inst/vanguard
-has/insights-pdfs/21_CIR_HAS21_HAS_FSreport.pdf.

167 three times more likely to invest in female CEOs: "Report: All In Women
in the VC Ecosystem," All Raise, 2019, https://www.allraise.org/assets/pitch
book_all_raise_2019_all_in_women_in_the_vc_ecosystem.pdf.

167 *accredited investor*: "Accredited Investor," U.S. Securities and Exchange Commission, https://www.sec.gov/education/capitalraising/building-blocks/accred
ited-investor.

168 less than .35 percent to Black women: Ty Heath, "VCs: This Is Why You're Not
Investing In Black Women, and Here's How to Change That," *Crunchbase*,
March 22, 2022, https://news.crunchbase.com/diversity/black-women-vc-di
versity-ty-heath-linkedin/.

168 SEC established a new rule: "SEC Adopts Rules to Permit Crowdfunding,"
U.S. Securities and Exchange Commission, October 30, 2015, https://www
.sec.gov/news/press-release/2015-249.

168 crowdfunding campaigns are 32 percent more successful: "Women Unbound:
Crowdfunding Unleashing Female Entrepreneurial Potential," Pricewater-
houseCoopers, July 2017, https://www.pwc.com/sg/en/publications/assets/wo
men-unbound-crowdfunding-report-2017.pdf.

Commandment 10: Bad Bitches Build Empires Together

178 reaching a five-year low: Jordan Rubio and Priyamvada Mathur, "An excep-
tional year for female founders still means a sliver of VC funding," PitchBook,
January 10, 2022, https://pitchbook.com/news/articles/female-founders-dash
board-2021-vc-funding-wrap-up.

181 Jo(h)n (5.3 percent) or David (4.5 percent) than there are women CEOs in total
(4.1 percent): Stefanie K. Johnson et al., "If There's Only One Woman in Your
Candidate Pool, There's Statistically No Chance She'll Be Hired," *Harvard
Business Review*, April 26, 2016, https://hbr.org/2016/04/if-theres-only-one
-woman-in-your-candidate-pool-theres-statistically-no-chance-shell-be-hired.

181 $650 billion annually: Amanda Novello, "The Cost of Inaction: How a Lack
of Family Care Policies Burdens the U.S. Economy and Families," National
Partnership for Women & Families, July 2021, https://www.nationalpartner
ship.org/our-work/resources/economic-justice/other/cost-of-inaction-lack-of
-family-care-burdens-families.pdf.

181 only 5 percent of healthcare leaders: "Delivered by Women, Led by Men: A
Gender and Equity Analysis of the Global Health and Social Workforce,"
Human Resources for Health Observer Series 24, World Health Organization,
2019.

181 80 percent more in annual healthcare costs: "Here's How Much Your Healthcare Costs Will Rise as You Age," RegisteredNursing.org, August 2022,
https://www.registerednursing.org/articles/healthcare-costs-by-age.

181 less than 20 percent of executive board members: Ratna Sahay et al., "Banking on Women Leaders: A Case for More?" International Monetary Fund, September 7, 2017, https://www.imf.org/en/Publications/WP/Issues/2017/09/07/Banking-on-Women-Leaders-A-Case-for-More-45221.

182 1.1 billion—remain outside the formal financial system: Ceyla Pazarbasioglu, "Women and finance: unlocking new sources of economic growth," World Bank Blogs, July 24, 2017, https://blogs.worldbank.org/voices/women-and-finance-unlocking-new-sources-economic-growth.

185 85 percent of consumer spending and influence 70 percent of household financial decisions: Krystle M. Davis, "20 Facts and Figures to Know When Marketing to Women," Forbes, May 13, 2019, https://www.forbes.com/sites/forbescontentmarketing/2019/05/13/20-facts-and-figures-to-know-when-marketing-to-women.

185 40 percent of US households: Sarah Jane Glynn, "Breadwinning Mothers Continue to Be the U.S. Norm," American Progress, May 10, 2019, https://www.americanprogress.org/article/breadwinning-mothers-continue-u-s-norm/.

186 biggest nations' economies in the next five years: Reenita Das, "The Rise of Sheconomy: Women's Increasing Impact on Business, Culture, and Healthcare," Frost & Sullivan, Jun 29, 2022, https://cnalifestyle.channelnewsasia.com/women/world-designed-men-gender-bias-stereotype-278011.

186 female crash test dummies: Keith Barry, "The Crash Test Bias: How Male-Focused Testing Puts Female Drivers at Risk," Consumer Reports, October 23, 2019, https://www.consumerreports.org/car-safety/crash-test-bias-how-male-focused-testing-puts-female-drivers-at-risk/.

186 considered a period tracker: Arielle Duhaime-Ross, "Apple Promised an Expansive Health App, So Why Can't I Track Menstruation?" The Verge, September 25, 2014, https://www.theverge.com/2014/9/25/6844021/apple-promised-an-expansive-health-app-so-why-cant-i-track.

186 their own biased data sets: Clementine Collett et al., "The Effects of AI on the Working Lives of Women," UNESCO, OECD, ID, 2022, https://publications.iadb.org/publications/english/document/The-Effects-of-AI-on-the-Working-Lives-of-Women.pdf.

187 more than 2x revenue per dollar invested: Katie Abouzahr et al., "Why Women-Owned Startups Are a Better Bet," Boston Consulting Group, June 6, 2018, https://www.bcg.com/publications/2018/why-women-owned-startups-are-better-bet.

188 Fortune 1000 companies led by female CEOs versus S&P 500: Pat Wechsler, "Women-led companies perform three times better than the S&P 500," Fortune, March 3, 2015, https://fortune.com/2015/03/03/women-led-companies-perform-three-times-better-than-the-sp-500/.

189 89 percent of new businesses: State of Women-Owned Businesses Report, "Woman-Owned Businesses Are Growing 2x Faster On Average Than All Businesses Nationwide," September 23, 2019, https://www.businesswire.com

/news/home/20190923005500/en/Woman-Owned-Businesses-Growing-2X -Faster-Average-Businesses.

189   Less than 2 percent of women-owned businesses have hit the million-dollar annual revenue mark: "2018 State of Women-Owned Business Report," Empower Women, 2018, https://www.empowerwomen.org/en/resources/docu ments/2019/01/the-2018-state-of-women-owned-business-report?lang=en.

189   menopause, a $600 billion market: Emma Hinchliffe, "Menopause is a $600 billion opportunity, report finds," *Fortune*, October 26, 2020, https://fortune .com/2020/10/26/menopause-startups-female-founders-fund-report/.

190   Eighty percent of women feel uncomfortable walking alone at night: "Perceptions of personal safety and experiences of harassment, Great Britain: 16 February to 13 March 2022," Opinions and Lifestyle Survey (OPN), Office For National Statistics, March 2022, https://www.ons.gov.uk/peoplepopulation andcommunity/crimeandjustice/bulletins/perceptionsofpersonalsafetyand experiencesofharassmentgreatbritain/16februaryto13march2022.

191   two out of ten cybersecurity professionals: "Women and Cybersecurity: Creating a More Inclusive Cyberspace," World Bank, May 26, 2022, https://www .worldbank.org/en/events/2022/04/26/women-and-cybersecurity-creating-a -more-inclusive-cyber-space.

191   cybersecurity market? A whopping $10.5 trillion: Steve Morgan, "Cybercrime to Cost the World $10.5 Trillion Annually by 2025," *Cybercrime Magazine*, November 13, 2020, https://cybersecurityventures.com/cybercrime-damage -costs-10-trillion-by-2025/.